DATE DUE

1st EDITION

Perspectives on Diseases and Disorders

Migraines

Mary E. Williams
Book Editor

PERSPECTIVES
On Diseases & Disorders

GALE
CENGAGE Learning

Detroit • New York • San Francisco • New Haven, Conn • Waterville, Maine • London

Christine Nasso, *Publisher*
Elizabeth Des Chenes, *Managing Editor*

© 2011 Greenhaven Press, a part of Gale, Cengage Learning

For more information, contact:
Greenhaven Press
27500 Drake Rd.
Farmington Hills, MI 48331-3535
Or you can visit our Internet site at gale.cengage.com

For product information and technology assistance, contact us at

Gale Customer Support, 1-800-877-4253
For permission to use material from this text or product, submit all requests online at www.cengage.com/permissions

Further permissions questions can be e-mailed to permissionrequest@cengage.com

Cover image Junial Enterprises/Shutterstock.com

LIBRARY OF CONGRESS CATALOGING-IN-PUBLICATION DATA

Migraines / Mary E. Williams, book editor.
    p. cm. -- (Perspectives on diseases and disorders)
  Includes bibliographical references and index.
  ISBN 978-0-7377-5254-0 (hardcover)
  1. Migraine. 2. Migraine--Treatment. 3. Migraine--Alternative treatment.
  I. Williams, Mary E., 1960-
  RC392.M617 2011
  616.8'4912--dc22

2011006296

Printed in the United States of America
1 2 3 4 5 6 7 15 14 13 12 11

CONTENTS

Foreword   7

Introduction   9

CHAPTER 1   Understanding Migraines

1. Migraines: An Overview   15

   *National Institute of Neurological
   Disorders and Stroke*

   A migraine occurs when certain kinds of
   brain neurons are activated, resulting in
   the constriction and dilation of brain blood
   vessels. This can cause a number of debilitating
   symptoms, including blurred vision, confusion,
   nausea, headache, and fatigue.

2. Migraines Are Connected to Sinus
   Headaches, Allergies, and Asthma   25

   Roger K. Cady

   Those who experience migraines are also
   more likely to suffer from allergies and asthma.
   Migraines are often misdiagnosed as sinus
   headaches.

3. Alcohol and Cigarettes Are Associated with
   Migraines in High Schoolers   32

   Obesity, Fitness & Wellness Week

   Teenagers who smoke and drink a lot of alcohol
   and coffee are more likely to have migraines.

4. Migraine Sufferers Face Stigma   36

   Ellin Holohan

   Migraine sufferers frequently experience
   criticism, ridicule, and rejection from family and
   employers when their condition prevents them
   from participating in ordinary activities.

CHAPTER 2   Issues and Controversies
                 Concerning Migraines

   1. New Drugs May Benefit Migraine Sufferers   41

   Anne Godlasky

   Newer migraine drugs, such as telcagepant,
   prevent the dilation of cerebral blood vessels.
   This can reduce or stop the headache pain that
   usually accompanies migraine.

   2. New Drugs Are Not Always the Best Choice
      for Migraine Sufferers   46

   Kerri Wachter

   Older migraine drugs are as effective at relieving
   symptoms as are the more recently developed
   drugs; however, the side effects and cost of the
   newer drugs may make them a bad choice for
   some patients.

   3. Most Migraine Sufferers Are Dissatisfied
      with Their Medications   52

   PR Newswire

   The majority of diagnosed migraine sufferers
   report that their prescribed medicine acts
   too slowly or that it is not effective for every
   migraine.

4. The Outlook for Migraine Sufferers Has
   Greatly Improved   58

   Barb Berggoetz

   Better remedies, including new drugs and
   drug combinations, alternative drug delivery
   systems, and various technological and nondrug
   therapies, are on the horizon for migraine
   patients.

5. Traditional Chinese Medicine Offers Effective
   Therapies for Migraine Sufferers   69

   Harry Hong

   A combination of Chinese herbs, acupuncture,
   dietary restrictions, and Qi Gong exercise therapy
   is an effective holistic approach to treating
   migraine.

6. The Effectiveness of Traditional Chinese
   Medicine Has Not Been Proved   77

   Stephen Barrett

   Authoritative research has not demonstrated that
   traditional Chinese medicine and acupuncture are
   effective against any disease.

7. Natural Remedies Are Effective
   Against Migraines   96

   Hillari Dowdle

   Migraine sufferers need not rely on drug
   treatments. A variety of natural remedies,
   including detoxes, acupuncture, massage,
   craniosacral therapy, biofeedback, and herbs
   and minerals can prevent or reduce painful
   symptoms.

8. Plastic Surgery Can Ease Migraines   **105**

Catherine Saint Louis

Plastic surgery on the "trigger points" of the temples, forehead, or back of the head can dramatically reduce the frequency of headaches for some migraine sufferers.

CHAPTER 3   Living with Migraines

1. Facing a Fear of Needles to Ease Migraine Pain   **112**

Gretchen Roberts

After years of suffering from migraines, this author faced her fear of needles and consulted an acupuncturist for treatment.

2. A Lifelong Journey with Migraines   **117**

"Nancy"

This grandmother shares her lifelong struggle with migraines, which started at a time when no medications for her attacks were available. She regrets having to miss out on so many things because of her disorder.

3. A Migraine Sufferer's Barometer Is in Her Head   **122**

Richard Brookhiser

This author explores his wife's history of migraine treatment. Her attacks, he notes, are often triggered by city noise and weather patterns.

Glossary   **126**

Chronology   **129**

Organizations to Contact   **132**

For Further Reading   **136**

Index   **138**

FOREWORD

"Medicine, to produce health, has to examine disease."
—Plutarch

Independent research on a health issue is often the first step to complement discussions with a physician. But locating accurate, well-organized, understandable medical information can be a challenge. A simple Internet search on terms such as "cancer" or "diabetes," for example, returns an intimidating number of results. Sifting through the results can be daunting, particularly when some of the information is inconsistent or even contradictory. The Greenhaven Press series Perspectives on Diseases and Disorders offers a solution to the often overwhelming nature of researching diseases and disorders.

From the clinical to the personal, titles in the Perspectives on Diseases and Disorders series provide students and other researchers with authoritative, accessible information in unique anthologies that include basic information about the disease or disorder, controversial aspects of diagnosis and treatment, and first-person accounts of those impacted by the disease. The result is a well-rounded combination of primary and secondary sources that, together, provide the reader with a better understanding of the disease or disorder.

Each volume in Perspectives on Diseases and Disorders explores a particular disease or disorder in detail. Material for each volume is carefully selected from a wide range of sources, including encyclopedias, journals, newspapers, nonfiction books, speeches, government documents, pamphlets, organization newsletters, and position papers. Articles in the first chapter provide an authoritative, up-to-date overview that covers symptoms, causes and effects, treatments, cures, and medical advances. The second chapter presents a substantial number of opposing viewpoints on controversial treatments and other current debates relating to the volume topic. The third chapter offers a variety of personal perspectives on the disease or disorder. Patients, doctors, caregivers, and loved ones represent just some of the voices found in this narrative chapter.

Each Perspectives on Diseases and Disorders volume also includes:

- An **annotated table of contents** that provides a brief summary of each article in the volume.

- An **introduction** specific to the volume topic.

- Full-color **charts and graphs** to illustrate key points, concepts, and theories.

- Full-color **photos** that show aspects of the disease or disorder and enhance textual material.

- **"Fast Facts"** that highlight pertinent additional statistics and surprising points.

- A **glossary** providing users with definitions of important terms.

- A **chronology** of important dates relating to the disease or disorder.

- An annotated list of **organizations to contact** for students and other readers seeking additional information.

- A **bibliography** of additional books and periodicals for further research.

- A detailed **subject index** that allows readers to quickly find the information they need.

Whether a student researching a disorder, a patient recently diagnosed with a disease, or an individual who simply wants to learn more about a particular disease or disorder, a reader who turns to Perspectives on Diseases and Disorders will find a wealth of information in each volume that offers not only basic information, but also vigorous debate from multiple perspectives.

INTRODUCTION

I n his 2009 memoir *A Brain Wider than the Sky*, migraine sufferer Andrew Levy relates in artful detail the experience of living with a serious chronic headache disorder. To depict the warning signs of one of his migraines, he writes, "There is no line between the migraine and worrying about the migraine as one lies awake at five in the morning. There is no difference between the first pinpricks of aura [a visual disturbance that precedes some migraines] and the first gray rays of dawn, either, since one looks like the other." After a few minutes, new symptoms emerge. Sounds and other sensations are intensified. "I can feel the shuffling under my brow, the blood and the nerves meditating, a little rush, a little constriction," Levy explains. "Then the first throb comes. . . . It starts from a point somewhere and pulsates, enlarges. By the third or fourth throb, a new pain appears, something after the throbs, like the afterimage on a television, a glow that grows fainter, until the next pulsation renews it. There's a density now, a consistency. I get up, and while the rest of my body feels normal, my head feels as if it is shedding pieces as it rises, like the trail of a comet."

At this point, Levy must act quickly if he hopes to subdue a debilitating headache. Ice packs and hot tea sometimes stop the pain within half an hour. Prescription painkillers provide relief on occasion, but reliance on them can actually lead to "rebound" headaches—migraines resulting from medication overuse. If he is unable to stop the pain, however, he may have to miss work, cancel an important outing, or struggle with the frustration of being unable to tend to his young son.

Levy's experience is all too familiar to about 36 million people in the United States. More than simply "bad headaches," migraine disorder is today recognized as a serious neurobiological disease with symptoms that may include sensory disturbances, dizziness, numbness, nausea, vomiting, and moderate to severe head pain lasting up to seventy-two hours. About 50 percent of people afflicted with migraine, however, have not been properly diagnosed, making this disorder one of the twenty-first century's silent epidemics. Identifying the affliction can be difficult because migraines vary in type and severity; moreover, migraine symptoms can resemble those of other disorders, such as sinus headaches, epilepsy, or strokes. In addition, many headache sufferers never consult a doctor about their pain and thus never learn that they may be experiencing migraines.

Headaches are grouped into two broad categories: primary and secondary. Primary headaches are self-contained—not a symptom of another disorder—while secondary headaches are caused by another medical condition (such as a viral infection, allergy, or tumor) or an injury. Identifying a headache as primary or secondary is an initial step in determining whether the pain is related to migraine or another headache disorder.

Primary headaches generally fall into three main types: tension-type headaches, migraines, and cluster headaches. According to the American Headache Society, tension-type headaches (TTH) are the most common, with up to 75 percent of the population experiencing them at some point. TTH symptoms include mild to moderate bilateral head pain of a pressing or tightening quality that lasts from thirty minutes to seven days. Such headaches may be accompanied by light or sound sensitivity, but they do not become more intense with physical activity, nor do they include nausea. Cluster headaches, on the other hand, are relatively rare, occurring in about 1 percent of the population. These headaches typically occur in hour-long attacks that occur several times a day for up to a week, with symptoms of severe unilateral pain around the eye or side of the head, along with nasal congestion, facial sweating, and restless agitation.

Migraines seem to reside in the middle of the continuum between tension-type headaches and cluster headaches. Like tension-type headaches, migraine symptoms may include sensitivity to light or sound. Unlike tension-type headaches, the pain of migraines is throbbing, usually restricted to one side of the head, frequently accompanied by nausea and vomiting, and typically intensified by physical movement. Although migraines share with cluster headaches the symptom of unilateral head pain, they do not have the same kind of episodic attack pattern.

While these conventionally defined distinctions between the three primary headache types may aid in properly diagnosing and treating migraine, some experts

Primary headaches fall into three categories: tension headaches, migraines, and cluster headaches. (**David Mack/ Photo Researchers, Inc.**)

maintain that overly rigid categorizations should be avoided. "At one time people thought that migraine was a disorder all its own and that tension-type headache was totally separate," says Dr. Ninan Mathew, director of the Houston Headache Clinic. "Now we realize that headaches are not that clear-cut."[1] Complicating matters, for example, is the fact that many headache sufferers experience both tension-type headaches and migraines. And an increasing number of researchers believe that all primary headache types are connected in some way to activity in the trigeminal nerve, a network of neurons that connect the jaws, face, and forehead to the brain. The differences between the headache types may stem from what stimulates this nerve and how it subsequently reacts.

According to scientists at the University of Maryland Medical Center, for example, various stimuli (stress, foods, odors, abnormal sleep patterns, weather changes) trigger the release of certain peptides (protein fragments) in migraineurs, people who get migraines. These peptides cause blood vessels to dilate, producing an inflammatory response that overexcites the trigeminal nerve, which then floods the brain with pain signals. In other words, the nervous systems of migraine sufferers seem to be primed to overreact to stimuli that most other people can tolerate. Furthermore, different individuals apparently have different thresholds at which "migraine responses" are set off. A migraineur likely has a low threshold for activating the trigeminal nerve, while a person who suffers an occasional tension-type headache has a much higher threshold, enabling him or her to avoid a full-blown migraine response most of the time.

No single model completely explains the migraine process, however. Researchers continue to investigate many other factors—altered levels of neurotransmitters (chemical messengers in the brain), magnesium deficiencies, abnormal intercellular calcium channels, hormonal fluctuations—which also play a role in the development of migraines. Through increased understanding, scientists hope to discover remedies that will prevent or more effectively treat this elusive disorder.

Perspectives on Diseases and Disorders: Migraines provides an accessible overview of a challenging neurobiological problem. Incorporating the perspectives of experts, health care providers, and migraine sufferers themselves, this volume provides opportunities to enhance awareness about an often unacknowledged illness.

Notes

1. Quoted in Christine Gorman and Alice Park, "The New Science of Headaches," *Time*, October 7, 2002.

CHAPTER 1

Understanding Migraines

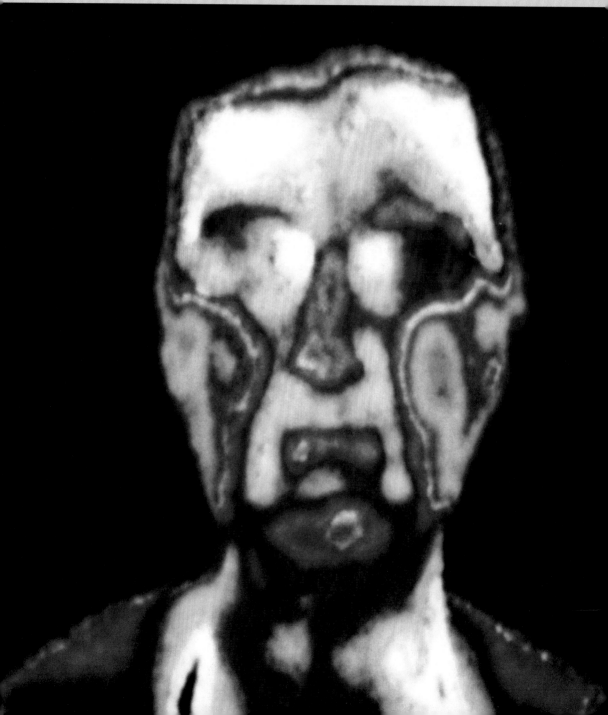

Migraines: An Overview

National Institute of Neurological Disorders and Stroke

The overactivation of neurons inside certain kinds of brain blood vessels can lead to an initial restriction of blood flow to the brain, which then causes other blood vessels to dilate and increase blood flow. The result is a migraine headache, an attack of up to three days in duration, with symptoms such as light and noise sensitivity, nausea, vomiting, throbbing pain on one side of the head, and fatigue. Certain kinds of foods, alcohol, stress, sleep disturbances, hormonal changes, and other environmental factors can trigger migraines. "Classic migraine" includes the sensation of light or other disturbances—an "aura"—before the onset of other symptoms, while the more common form of migraine occurs without an aura. Treatments for migraine include a variety of drugs and natural supplements that can relieve symptoms and prevent future attacks. This selection is excerpted from an educational document drafted by the National Institute of Neurological Disorders and Stroke, an arm of the National Institutes of Health within the US Department of Health and Human Services.

Photo on facing page. Shown here is a thermogram of the head of a patient with a severe migraine. The colors show temperature ranging from cold (black) through normal (green) to hot (red, yellow, and white). Migraine-related hot spots are shown around base of the neck, near the eyes, and around the brain. (Dr. G. Raviley/ Photo Researchers, Inc.)

SOURCE: National Institute of Neurological Disorders and Stroke (NINDS), "Headache: Hope Through Research," August 13, 2010. www.ninds.nih.gov.

If you suffer from migraine headaches, you're not alone. About 12 percent of the U.S. population experience migraines, one form of *vascular* headaches. Vascular headaches are characterized by throbbing and pulsating pain caused by the activation of nerve fibers that reside within the wall of brain blood vessels traveling within the meninges [membranes surrounding the brain]. Blood vessels narrow, temporarily, which decreases the flow of blood and oxygen to the brain. This causes other blood vessels to open wider and increase blood flow.

Migraines involve recurrent attacks of moderate to severe pain that is throbbing or pulsing and often strikes one side of the head. Untreated attacks last from 4 to 72 hours. Other common symptoms are increased sensitivity to light, noise, and odors; and nausea and vomiting. Routine physical activity, movement, or even coughing or sneezing can worsen the headache pain.

Migraines occur most frequently in the morning, especially upon waking. Some people have migraines at predictable times, such as before menstruation or on weekends following a stressful week of work. Many people feel exhausted or weak following a migraine but are usually symptom-free between attacks.

A number of different factors can increase your risk of having a migraine. These factors, which trigger the headache process, vary from person to person and include sudden changes in weather or environment, too much or not enough sleep, strong odors or fumes, emotion, stress, overexertion, loud or sudden noises, motion sickness, low blood sugar, skipped meals, tobacco, depression, anxiety, head trauma, hangover, some medications, hormonal changes, and bright or flashing lights. Medication overuse or missed doses may also cause headaches. In some 50 percent of migraine sufferers, foods or ingredients can trigger headaches. These include aspartame, caffeine (or caffeine withdrawal), wine and other types

Migraines: The Role of Blood Vessels

When certain neurons in the brain are overactive, the resulting constriction and dilation of blood vessels can cause pain and other symptoms associated with migraine.

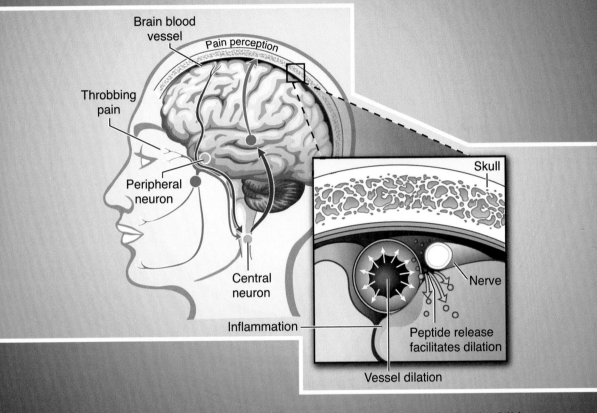

Brain blood vessel

Pain perception

Throbbing pain

Peripheral neuron

Central neuron

Skull

Nerve

Inflammation

Peptide release facilitates dilation

Vessel dilation

Taken from: *Migraine Relief*, "Migraine Causes—Things You Should Know," September 3, 2009. http://migrainerelief.info.

of alcohol, chocolate, aged cheeses, monosodium glutamate, some fruits and nuts, fermented or pickled goods, yeast, and cured or processed meats. Keeping a diet journal will help identify food triggers.

Who Gets Migraines?

Migraines occur in both children and adults, but affect adult women three times more often than men. There is evidence that migraines are genetic, with most migraine sufferers having a family history of the disorder. They also frequently occur in people who have other medical conditions. Depression, anxiety, bipolar disorder, sleep disorders, and epilepsy are more common in individuals with migraine than in the general population. Migraine sufferers—in particular those individuals who have pre-migraine symptoms referred to as aura—have a slightly increased risk of having a stroke.

Migraine in women often relates to changes in hormones. The headaches may begin at the start of the first menstrual cycle or during pregnancy. Most women see improvement after menopause, although surgical removal of the ovaries usually worsens migraines. Women with migraine who take oral contraceptives may experience changes in the frequency and severity of attacks, while women who do not suffer from headaches may develop migraines as a side effect of oral contraceptives.

Phases of Migraine

Migraine is divided into four phases, all of which may be present during the attack:

- *Premonitory* symptoms occur up to 24 hours prior to developing a migraine. These include food cravings, unexplained mood changes (depression or euphoria), uncontrollable yawning, fluid retention, or increased urination.
- *Aura.* Some people will see flashing or bright lights or what looks like heat waves immediately prior to or during the migraine, while others may experience muscle weakness or the sensation of being touched or grabbed.
- *Headache.* A migraine usually starts gradually and builds in intensity. It is possible to have migraine without a headache.
- *Postdrome* (following the headache). Individuals are often exhausted or confused following a migraine.

The postdrome period may last up to a day before people feel healthy.

Types of Migraine

The two major types of migraine are:

- *Migraine with aura*, previously called classic migraine, includes visual disturbances and other neurological symptoms that appear about 10 to 60 minutes before the actual headache and usually last no more than an hour. Individuals may temporarily lose part or all of their vision. The aura may occur without headache pain, which can strike at any time. Other classic symptoms include trouble speaking; an abnormal sensation, numbness, or muscle weakness on one side of the body; a tingling sensation

Migraines occur in both children and adults, and they affect women three times more often than men. (Christina Pedrazzini/ Photo Researchers, Inc.)

in the hands or face, and confusion. Nausea, loss of appetite, and increased sensitivity to light, sound, or noise may precede the headache.

- *Migraine without aura*, or common migraine, is the more frequent form of migraine. Symptoms include headache pain that occurs without warning and is usually felt on one side of the head, along with nausea, confusion, blurred vision, mood changes, fatigue, and increased sensitivity to light, sound, or noise.

Other types of migraine include:

- *Abdominal migraine* mostly affects young children and involves moderate to severe pain in the middle of the abdomen lasting 1 to 72 hours, with little or no headache. Additional symptoms include nausea, vomiting, and loss of appetite. Many children who develop abdominal migraine will have migraine headaches later in life.
- *Basilar-type migraine* mainly affects children and adolescents. It occurs most often in teenage girls and may be associated with their menstrual cycle. Symptoms include partial or total loss of vision or double vision, dizziness and loss of balance, poor muscle coordination, slurred speech, a ringing in the ears, and fainting. The throbbing pain may come on suddenly and is felt on both sides at the back of the head.
- *Hemiplegic migraine* is a rare but severe form of migraine that causes temporary paralysis—sometimes lasting several days—on one side of the body prior to or during a headache. Symptoms such as vertigo, a pricking or stabbing sensation, and problems seeing, speaking, or swallowing may begin prior to the headache pain and usually stop shortly thereafter. When it runs in families the disorder is called Familial Hemiplegic Migraine (FHM). Though rare, at least three distinct genetic forms of FHM have been identified. These genetic mutations make the brain

more sensitive or excitable, most likely by increasing brain levels of a chemical called glutamate.

- *Menstrually-related migraine* affects women around the time of their period, although most women with menstrually-related migraine also have migraines at other times of the month. Symptoms may include migraine without aura (which is much more common during menses than migraine with aura), pulsing pain on one side of the head, nausea, vomiting, and increased sensitivity to sound and light.
- *Migraine without headache* is characterized by visual problems or other aura symptoms, nausea, vomiting, and constipation, but without head pain. Headache specialists have suggested that fever, dizziness, and/or unexplained pain in a particular part of the body could also be possible types of headache-free migraine.
- *Ophthalmoplegic migraine* is an uncommon form of migraine with head pain, along with a droopy eyelid, large pupil, and double vision that may last for weeks, long after the pain is gone.
- *Retinal migraine* is a condition characterized by attacks of visual loss or disturbances in one eye. These attacks, like the more common visual auras, are usually associated with migraine headaches.
- *Status migrainosus* is a rare and severe type of acute migraine in which disabling pain and nausea can last 72 hours or longer. The pain and nausea may be so intense that sufferers need to be hospitalized.

Migraine Treatment

Migraine treatment is aimed at relieving symptoms and preventing additional attacks. Quick steps to ease symptoms may include napping or resting with eyes closed in a quiet, darkened room; placing a cool cloth or ice pack on the forehead, and drinking lots of fluid, particularly if the migraine is accompanied by vomiting. Small amounts of caffeine may help relieve symptoms during a migraine's early stages.

Drug therapy for migraine is divided into acute and preventive treatment. Acute or "abortive" medications are taken as soon as symptoms occur to relieve pain and restore function. Preventive treatment involves taking medicines daily to reduce the severity of future attacks or keep them from happening. The U.S. Food and Drug Administration (FDA) has approved a variety of drugs for these treatment methods. Headache drug use should be monitored by a physician, since some drugs may cause side effects.

Acute treatment for migraine may include any of the following drugs.

- Triptan drugs increase levels of the neurotransmitter *serotonin* in the brain. Serotonin causes blood vessels to constrict and lowers the pain threshold. Triptans—the preferred treatment for migraine— ease moderate to severe migraine pain and are available as tablets, nasal sprays, and injections.
- Ergot derivative drugs bind to serotonin receptors on nerve cells and decrease the transmission of pain messages along nerve fibers. They are most effective during the early stages of migraine and are available as nasal sprays and injections.
- Non-prescription analgesics or over-the-counter drugs such as ibuprofen, aspirin, or acetaminophen can ease the pain of less severe migraine headache.
- Combination analgesics involve a mix of drugs such as acetaminophen plus caffeine and/or a narcotic for migraine that may be resistant to simple analgesics.
- Nonsteroidal anti-inflammatory drugs can reduce inflammation and alleviate pain.
- Nausea relief drugs can ease queasiness brought on by various types of headache.
- Narcotics are prescribed briefly to relieve pain. These drugs should not be used to treat chronic headaches.

Taking headache relief drugs more than three times a week may lead to *medication overuse headache* (previously called rebound headache), in which the initial headache is relieved temporarily but reappears as the drug wears off. Taking more of the drug to treat the new headache leads to progressively shorter periods of pain relief and results in a pattern of recurrent chronic headache. Headache pain ranges from moderate to severe and may occur with nausea or irritability. It may take weeks for these headaches to end once the drug is stopped.

Everyone with migraine needs effective treatment at the time of the headaches. Some people with frequent and severe migraine need preventive medications. In general, prevention should be considered if migraines occur one or more times weekly, or if migraines are less frequent but disabling. Preventive medicines are also recommended for individuals who take symptomatic headache treatment more than three times a week. Physicians will also recommend that a migraine sufferer take one or more preventive medications two to three months to assess drug effectiveness, unless intolerable side effects occur.

FAST FACT

According to the World Health Organization, three thousand migraines occur every day for each million people in the general population.

Preventive Medications

Several preventive medicines for migraine were initially marketed for conditions other than migraine.

- Anticonvulsants may be helpful for people with other types of headaches in addition to migraine. Although they were originally developed for treating epilepsy, these drugs increase levels of certain neurotransmitters and dampen pain impulses.
- Beta-blockers are drugs for treating high blood pressure that are often effective for migraine.
- Calcium channel blockers are medications that are also used to treat high blood pressure and help to stabilize blood vessel walls. These drugs appear to work

by preventing the blood vessels from either narrowing or widening, which affects blood flow to the brain.

• Antidepressants are drugs that work on different chemicals in the brain; their effectiveness in treating migraine is not directly related to their effect on mood. Antidepressants may be helpful for individuals with other types of headaches because they increase the production of serotonin and may also affect levels of other chemicals, such as norepinephrine and dopamine. The types of antidepressants used for migraine treatment include selective serotonin reuptake inhibitors, serotonin and norepinephrine reuptake inhibitors, and tricyclic antidepressants (which are also used to treat tension-type headaches).

Natural treatments for migraine include riboflavin (vitamin B2), magnesium, coenzyme Q10, and butterbur.

Non-drug therapy for migraine includes biofeedback and relaxation training, both of which help individuals cope with or control the development of pain and the body's response to stress.

Lifestyle changes that reduce or prevent migraine attacks in some individuals include exercising, avoiding food and beverages that trigger headaches, eating regularly scheduled meals with adequate hydration, stopping certain medications, and establishing a consistent sleep schedule. Obesity increases the risk of developing chronic daily headache, so a weight loss program is recommended for obese individuals.

Migraines Are Connected to Sinus Headaches, Allergies, and Asthma

Roger K. Cady

In the following selection physician Roger K. Cady explores the relationship between a few disorders that affect different defense systems within the human body. Asthma, he points out, results from a disruption to systems that protect the lungs, while allergies and sinus headaches emerge from mechanisms that defend the skin or sinuses. Migraines occur in those who have extrasensitive nervous systems. These disorders have varying levels of comorbidity; that is, having one of them increases the chance of having another one or more of the others. For example, at least 40 percent of people who suffer from migraines also suffer from allergies, and they are also twice as likely to experience asthma. What connects all of these disorders, Cady explains, is that they each emerge when one of the body's defense mechanisms overreacts to a potential threat. Cady is the director of the Headache Care Center in Springfield, Missouri.

SOURCE: Roger K. Cady, "Sinus Headaches, Allergies, Asthma, and Migraine: More than a Casual Relationship?," *Headache: The Newsletter of ACHE,* American Headache Society, November 2008. Reprinted by permission.

In order to survive, all living organisms must be able to separate themselves from their environment. They must be able to absorb nutrients from that environment, while at the same time protect themselves from injury and contamination. To ensure that we live safely within our environment, nature has evolved complex safeguards involving the nervous system, endocrine (hormonal) system, and immune system. As part of this defense system, each portal of entry into the human body has a sophisticated mechanism in place to provide this protection. While most of the time these defense mechanisms function flawlessly, there is the potential for problems; and several important disorders, including migraine, asthma, and allergies, may reflect disruptions of these mechanisms. Disruption of the defense mechanisms designed to protect the lung can result in asthma. If those in the skin or sinus go awry, allergies can result, and if those involving the nervous system are disrupted, migraine can result.

Sensitive Systems for Better and for Worse

People with migraine inherit a nervous system that is more sensitive to change than those without migraine. This nervous system evolved to be highly vigilant of its environment. When the migrainous nervous system is functioning well, this vigilance is often reflected in positive ways. For example, people with migraine are often well-organized, perceptive, and successful in school and artistic activities. This heightened vigilance may also be why migraine sufferers tend to be light sleepers and more emotionally vulnerable. However, if the nervous system perceives a threat from either the external or internal environment, the nervous system response can be an attack of migraine.

People born with asthma inherit a respiratory or airway system that is more sensitive and vigilant of its environment than those without asthma. When an asthmatic airway is threatened, it can respond dramatically by narrowing too much and creating an inflammatory response in this defense perimeter. This results in wheezing and shortness of breath.

In a similar fashion, people with allergies respond in a variety of ways when their systems are threatened. The most dramatic is an *anaphylactic* reaction. This is the type of reaction noted rarely with a bee sting or an injection of penicillin and can be fatal. More commonly, allergic individuals develop sinus or skin symptoms that can vary considerably in severity. Seasonal allergies are likely the most common allergic condition. Symptoms generally consist of nasal congestion and discharge, eye irritation, and sometimes headache. Allergies can also be closely associated with asthma.

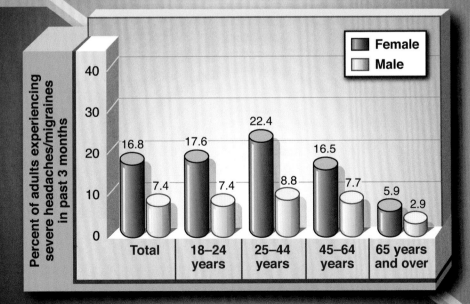

Adults Aged 18 and Older with Severe Headaches or Migraines, 2007

Percent of adults experiencing severe headaches/migraines in past 3 months

Female
Male

	Total	18–24 years	25–44 years	45–64 years	65 years and over
Female	16.8	17.6	22.4	16.5	5.9
Male	7.4	7.4	8.8	7.7	2.9

Taken from: Centers for Disease Control and Prevention, National Center for Health Statistics, and National Health Interview Survey, 2009.

Links Between Diverse Disorders

Observations that link these seemingly diverse disorders together include the fact that they are common in the general population, genetic factors appear to be important for all of them, each can be triggered by internal or external threats, and each represents an over-response or exaggerated response of the very mechanisms that nature designed to protect us. Given these similarities, it is not surprising that if you inherit one of these disorders, you have a greater likelihood of inheriting one or more of the others. When conditions are more likely to occur together than what is found by chance alone in the general population they are called comorbid conditions. In the recent American Migraine Study II, 40%–70% of respondents with migraine had comorbid allergies. Other studies have reported that people with migraine are 2 to 3.5 times more likely to have comorbid asthma, especially if they have a parent with migraine and asthma.

Unraveling the relationships these comorbid disorders have to each other poses many interesting questions. For example, can allergies or asthma trigger migraine? Clearly, these associations appear to be popular beliefs. For example, it has long been assumed that allergies are part of sinus disease and that sinus disease, in turn, results in "sinus headache." In fact, most participants in the American Migraine Study II who had diagnosed migraine also reported having "sinus headaches." However, whether sinus headache and migraine are distinct headache disorders or related to one another is a matter of debate.

Several studies in the medical literature have evaluated a group or population of people who reported they had recurrent attacks of sinus headaches. These patients may be either self diagnosed as having sinus headache or incorrectly diagnosed by a physician as having sinus

> **FAST FACT**
>
> The journal *Neurology* reports that 64 percent of migraine patients in the United Kingdom and 77 percent of those in the United States never receive a correct medical diagnosis for their headaches.

headache. Either way, many of these people actually have migraine and not sinus headache. The reason there is confusion between sinus headache and migraine is that pain that occurs near or around the sinuses may be incorrectly assumed to be sinus, based on this location. However, the truth is that migraine also presents with pain in the forehead and around the eye and therefore may be thought to be sinus. Also these studies tell us that if you have pain that appears to be sinus headache, you should see your doctor and ask for a full diagnosis of your headaches. This is very important because treatment of sinus headache or sinusitis differs significantly from treatment for migraine.

Important Facts About Sinus Headache and Migraine

- Most sinus headache is misdiagnosed, and these patients may have migraine.
- Sinus headaches are not normally disabling, and migraine headaches are.
- True sinus headache or sinusitis is associated with a pus-like or purulent nasal discharge that represents a potential infection in the sinuses. Migraine may be associated with watery eyes and runny nose, but the fluid is clear.
- Sinusitis as a disorder may be associated with headache, but these headaches may differ from migraine.
- Patients with sinusitis may also have migraine.

Important Facts About Allergic Rhinitis and Migraine

Allergic rhinitis is a histamine-driven response to an allergen and when exposed to this allergen, the nasal passage becomes inflamed and irritated resulting in a "runny nose." Histamine release has also been suggested to be involved in triggering migraine headaches. Allergic rhinitis can be screened for with simple skin testing at your allergist's office or even in some primary care offices. Many people who

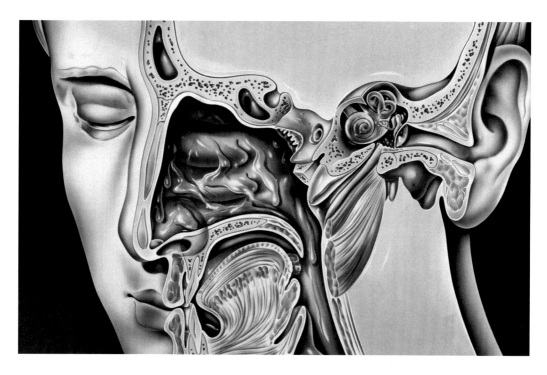

This image shows the effects of allergic rhinitis on the sinuses. Mucus is produced in the mucous membrane (red) that lines the nasal cavity and facial sinuses. The release of histamines is believed to cause some migraines. (John Bavosi/Photo Researchers, Inc.)

have allergic rhinitis also have migraine. People with allergic rhinitis have a general histamine response to something they are allergic to.

- Histamine release may also be involved in triggering headache, specifically migraine.
- People with allergic rhinitis are more than 10 times more likely to have migraine.
- Accurate diagnoses and treatment of allergic rhinitis will be an important part in reducing the risk of migraine.
- Learning how to treat each condition individually should improve overall care and reduce disability of migraine associated with allergic rhinitis.

Important Facts About Asthma and Migraine

The relationship between migraine and asthma is equally confusing. Clearly, there is some overlap in the risk or triggering factors for asthma and migraine—for example, stress and certain environmental triggers or allergens. Often migraine sufferers with asthma report that both asthma and migraine can worsen at the same time, and occasionally one seems to lead to the other. In one study, patients with asthma were 1.5 times more likely to also have migraine.

- Asthma may be triggered by a number of different allergens or environmental triggers that also may lead to other airway conditions such as allergic rhinitis.
- Airway conditions including asthma, allergic rhinitis, or sinusitis all may be associated with headache.
- Diagnosing the specific headaches associated with airway conditions is important to ensure that treatment is successful. For example, some over-the-counter allergy medicines may also lead to a worsening of headache in some patients, especially if taken frequently.
- Asthma may be associated or comorbid with migraine and a full diagnosis of each condition is needed.
- Identifying potential triggers for asthma is important for reducing the risk of an attack and the risk of triggering a migraine.

Accurate Diagnosis Is Crucial

Throughout the literature there are many reports that headaches occur in patients with airway symptoms, including sinusitis, allergic rhinitis or even asthma. The link between these conditions and headache is not well understood, but based on their frequent association, they may be comorbid conditions. To improve the chances of successful treatment, accurate diagnosis for each condition is critical because a single approach is unlikely to be successful in treating both conditions. Additionally, identifying those patients who are incorrectly diagnosed is also important when developing a treatment plan.

Alcohol and Cigarettes Are Associated with Migraines in High Schoolers

Obesity, Fitness & Wellness Week

A German study of students between the ages of fourteen and twenty found that alcohol and coffee consumption, cigarette smoking, and physical inactivity lead to an increased number of migraines in youths. As these are modifiable risk factors, research leader Astrid Milde-Busch recommends the development of programs to educate youths about headache-triggering behaviors. This article was prepared by the editors of *Obesity, Fitness & Wellness Week*.

A novel study by German researchers reported that alcohol consumption and cigarette smoking were associated with increased migraines and tension-type headaches (TTH) in high school students. Coffee drinking and physical inactivity were associated specifically with migraines. . . .

Prior studies have indicated that headache is one of the most frequently reported health complaints in adoles-

SOURCE: *Obesity, Fitness & Wellness Week,* "Alcohol Use and Smoking Are Associated with Headaches in High Schoolers," June 26, 2010. Reprinted by permission.

cents with 5%–15% of this age group suffering from migraine and 15%–25% with TTH. Modifiable risk factors, such as alcohol use, cigarette smoking and coffee drinking which have been associated with headache in adults, have not been fully explored in a youth population.

The German Study

Astrid Milde-Busch, Ph.D., and colleagues at the Ludwig-Maximilians-University in Munich, Germany, invited 1,260 students in grades 10 and 11 (aged 14–20) from eleven area public schools to participate in the study. The students were asked to fill out a questionnaire on headache and associated lifestyle factors. Students were asked: "Did you have headache during the last seven days/three months/six months?" and were classified as headache sufferers if the response was positive. Furthermore, migraine and TTH were differentiated by questions regarding headache characteristics and symptoms. The questionnaire also inquired about diet and lifestyle (e.g. "Do you daily have breakfast before you go to school?"; "How much beer, wine and cocktails do you normally drink?"; "How much coffee do you normally drink?"; "Do you smoke?").

> **FAST FACT**
>
> The chemical compounds tyramine and histamine, contained in many red wines and beers, are known to provoke migraines.

Research results show 83.1% of students reported headache at least once during the previous six months with 10.2% reporting migraine; 48.7% citing TTH; and 19.8% having combined migraine plus TTH. For diet, 28.4% of students never had breakfast; 16.5% did not eat a daily break meal (snack); and only 24.0% had a daily warm lunch. Researchers found that 22.3% of students consumed less than 1 liter (4.23 8 ounce cups) of non-alcoholic drinks per day. Alcohol consumption, however, was widespread among students in the study with 38.5%, 18.6%, and 25.3% drinking beer, wine, and cocktails at least once per week, respectively.

A German study revealed that behaviors such as coffee and alcohol consumption, cigarette smoking, and physical inactivity have led to an increase in the number of migraines among teens.
(Véronique Burger/Photo Researchers, Inc.)

Results also showed that 73.3% of participants reported never smoking and 43.4% [of] students noted that they did not drink coffee.

Factors Associated with Migraine

The authors found that a high consumption of alcoholic drinks and coffee, smoking, and lack of physical activity were significantly associated with migraine plus TTH episodes. There was a significant association of coffee drinking and physical inactivity with migraine. "Our study confirms, adolescents with any type of headache might benefit from regular physical activity and low consumption of alcoholic drinks," commented Dr. Milde-Busch. "In teens suffering from migraine a low coffee consumption should also be suggested." Skipping meals or insufficient fluid intake was not associated with any type of headache.

According to the Centers for Disease Control and Prevention (CDC), 75% of high school students in the U.S. have had one or more alcoholic drinks during their lifetime (2007). A 2004 report by the World Health Organization (WHO) notes that alcohol consumption by those under 20 varies by country and "a trend of increased drinking to intoxication." Cigarette smoking is another modifiable risk factor in which youths engage and a 2002 WHO report estimated about 1 in every 5 teens worldwide (aged 13) smoke. "A great number of teens are engaging in activities such as drinking and smoking which can trigger headaches," concluded Dr. Milde-Busch. "Intervention studies that assess psycho-education programs to educate youths about headache-triggering behaviors are recommended."

Migraine Sufferers Face Stigma

Ellin Holohan

Migraine sufferers frequently face misunderstanding and skepticism about their condition from relatives, coworkers, and employers, writes Ellin Holohan in the following selection. Because migraine is an invisible condition, some people presume that those who claim to have migraines are lying or exaggerating about their pain to avoid work and other events. But migraine is a real biological disorder with symptoms severe enough to keep sufferers from being able to work or engage in ordinary activities, Holohan says. Researchers hope that increased public awareness about the disease will help reduce the burden and stigma that can leave migraine sufferers feeling isolated and ostracized. Holohan is a reporter for HealthDay, a medical news service headquartered in Norwalk, Connecticut.

People who suffer from chronic migraine headaches feel more rejected, ridiculed, and ostracized by family, friends, and employers than patients with other neurological troubles, a new study contends.

SOURCE: Ellin Holohan, "For Migraine Sufferers, Stigma Adds to Burden," HealthDay, June 25, 2010. Reprinted by permission.

And the more severe the condition is, the more stigma victims experience, the Philadelphia researchers say.

Lead author Dr. Jung E. Park, a neurological resident at Thomas Jefferson University Hospital, said that people are often skeptical of claims about migraine headaches because they are intangible. "You can't see it, so people don't understand the condition," she said, and co-workers and employers sometimes "think the person is trying to get more time off for something unimportant" because they "don't think the pain and suffering is real."

Many people with migraine [migraineurs] experienced "separation, exclusion and rejection in their relationships with family and friends when their condition prevented them from fully engaging in family and social events," the study found.

The greater the stigma, the lower the quality of life for migraine sufferers as measured by absence from work, family events and social life, according to the study, which the authors say is the first to look at migraine and stigma.

The Stigma Scale

The findings are to be presented this week [in late June 2010] at the annual meeting of the American Headache Society (AHS) in Los Angeles.

The study relied on the Stigma Scale for Chronic Illness, an instrument developed at Northwestern University, to compare the stigma experienced by chronic migraine sufferers with people who have episodic (non-chronic) migraine, stroke, epilepsy, Parkinson's, Alzheimer's, and amyotrophic lateral sclerosis (ALS, or Lou Gehrig's disease). The scale measures factors such as how often people feel criticized, misunderstood or ostracized for having an illness.

The scores of 246 adult migraine sufferers—all outpatients at the hospital's Jefferson Headache Clinic—were compared to those of people with the other neurological conditions. Half of the people with migraine had the headaches episodically, while the other half suffered from chronic migraine.

Those with chronic migraine scored significantly higher on the stigma scale than either people with episodic migraine or those with other neurological conditions, Park said.

The stigma can reach deep into migraineurs' personal lives. For example, Park said she has known married couples who divorced because migraines were misunderstood.

"A husband felt that things weren't the same when his wife couldn't have sexual intercourse or maybe take care of the children as much as she once did," said Park. "When something impacts functioning like this, and is not well understood, we tend to stigmatize."

A Real Biological Disorder

AHS president Dr. David Dodick said the research was important because people with migraines have been strongly stereotyped in the past as "high-strung, neurotic women who can't handle daily stress."

Three times as many women as men get migraine, noted Dodick, "likely due to the effect of fluctuating estrogen levels on brain excitability" during the reproductive years.

And while onlookers may sometimes be skeptical about the reality of migraine, migraine "is a real biological disorder," Dodick said. Migraineurs typically become sensitive to light and sound, and often suffer from nausea, diarrhea, and changes in blood pressure. These conditions can persist even when no headache is present.

While migraines are genetically based in many cases, people who get them tend to be less-educated and have relatively low incomes because their functioning is so affected by the disease, Dodick said.

FAST FACT

Science Daily reports that US employers lose 157 million workdays to migraines each year.

A young woman displays the various medications she takes for chronic migraine headaches. Female migraine sufferers have been stereotyped as high-strung and neurotic. (Janet Hostetter/AP Images)

"There is such a thing as being 'present' at work but not really being able to function well," noted Dodick, a professor of neurology at the Mayo Clinic in Scottsdale, Ariz. Many migraine sufferers lose their jobs because of their illness, he said, and because of stigma "many people are afraid to admit they get migraines." Sufferers can often become depressed, he added.

However, the new research "starts a conversation and is a step toward banishing the stigma and allowing individuals with migraine not to suffer in silence, and hopefully eliminates the burden, as they are already burdened enough by the disease," said Dodick. "Hopefully, this research will help them come out of the closet."

CHAPTER 2

Issues and Controversies
Concerning Migraines

New Drugs May Benefit Migraine Sufferers

Anne Godlasky

New drugs and treatments may soon provide marked relief for migraine patients, reports Anne Godlasky in the selection that follows. One drug, telcagepant, prevents the activation of neurons that signal cerebral blood vessels to dilate. This blood vessel dilation is the primary cause of headache pain in migraine sufferers, Godlasky points out. Another treatment, the transcranial magnetic stimulator, would help to stop the visual aura that some migraine patients experience before the onset of other symptoms. Researchers assert that interrupting this aura can reduce or prevent pain. Godlasky is a reporter for the daily newspaper *USA Today*.

Headaches distract. Migraines can debilitate. Nearly 30 million Americans suffer from the throbbing pain, costing employers about $13 billion a year from missed workdays and impaired work function, according to research reported in the *Archives of Internal Medicine*.

Photo on facing page. A mother comforts her young daughter, who is experiencing the onset of a migraine headache. (© INSADCO Photography/Alamy)

SOURCE: Anne Godlasky, "New Ways to Mitigate Migraines," *USA Today,* November 4, 2008, p. 10 D. Reprinted by permission.

"You can be out for three days—lie there and not move, feel nauseous but not throw up—it's incapacitating," says Jeanne Safer, 61, of New York, a psychotherapist who has had regular migraines for about a decade.

But new treatments in the pipeline may help control the pain. Some "exciting" new drugs are coming into the headache field, says Alan Rapoport, a UCLA [University of California at Los Angeles] professor of neurology who has studied headaches for 35 years.

The Trigeminal Nerve System

Scientists still haven't agreed on a single cause of migraines, although genetic and hormonal factors and some environmental triggers often play a part.

But wherever a migraine starts—whether with malfunctioning nerve cells deep in the brain stem or hyperexcited neurons in the cerebral cortex—it sets off something called the trigeminal nerve system, which carries sensory information from the face, head and meninges (membranes covering the brain and spinal cord) to the brain stem.

During a migraine, the trigeminal nerve releases a peptide called CGRP (calcitonin gene-related peptide), which causes dilation of blood vessels and increased pain signaling. A drug that would prevent the peptide from activating the neurons is in final trials: Mercks [a pharmaceutical company] telcagepant. Its latest study showed that about 55% of patients had marked pain relief, and 23% were pain-free after two hours, significantly better than placebo patients. Merck plans to apply for Food and Drug Administration [FDA] approval for telcagepant next year [in 2009]. Other companies are starting trials on similar drugs.

New Drug May Eclipse Triptans

Interest among migraine specialists stems from evidence that these drugs are at least as effective as triptans, the most commonly prescribed class of migraine drug, writes Stephen Silberstein in the October [2008] issue of the *Lancet*.

Triptans were considered a major breakthrough when they arrived about 15 years ago. But unlike triptans, the new drugs don't constrict vessels, so they may be safer for patients with high blood pressure, high cholesterol and a variety of vascular diseases.

Symptoms of Different Kinds of Headaches

Migraine

- Pulsing or throbbing pain
- Sensitivity to light and noise
- Nausea or vomiting
- Often on one side of the head
- Aggravated by routine physical activity
- Lasts four hours to three days

Tension Headache

- Vise-like pressure or ache around the head; no throbbing
- Tightness in the neck
- Occurs in forehead, temples, or back of the head and neck
- Lasts thirty minutes to seven days

Sinus Headache

- Pressure around the nose and cheeks and under the eyes
- Usually accompanied by a fever and infection or allergies

Cluster Headache

- Affects less than 1 percent of population—mostly men
- Also called suicide headache
- Piercing pain on one side
- Often accompanied by eye pain or watering, runny nose
- Lasts thirty to forty-five minutes in clusters in the same day
- Can go on for weeks or months, then stop for months or years

Taken from: National Headache Foundation, www.headaches.org.

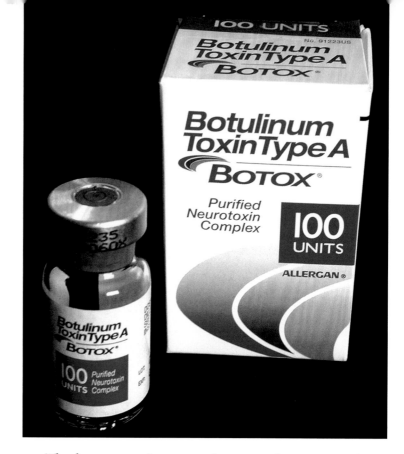

Migraine sufferers who received Botox treatments had fewer days with headaches than those who got dummy injections, according to two studies done by the drug maker Allergan. (Scott Carmazine/Photo Researchers, Inc.)

The heart warnings on triptans make some patients nervous, including Safer. But because she has about 15 headaches a month, she's settled on taking her triptan, Maxalt, in addition to Botox injections every 2 1/2 months and—if the pain is unbearable and she has used up her medication—shots of lidocaine, an anesthetic. Patients who received Botox had fewer days with headaches compared with those who got dummy injections, according to two studies funded by drugmaker Allergan. Botox is FDA-approved for cosmetic use, and Allergan announced in September [2008], that it would seek approval for use against migraines.

Addressing Migraine Aura

Safer's doctor, Alexander Mauskop, also gets migraines, and like about 30% of migraines patients, pain is sometimes preceded by a visual aura. "You see flickering lights, spots, zigzags, sometimes in color," he says.

For patients who experience aura, which many scientists believe is caused by an electrical abnormality called cortical spreading depression, a new device may stop it before it signals pain.

"If you have a fire that starts in a forest, then the fire would spread from one tree to another until it reaches your house," says Yousef Mohammad, a professor of neurology at Ohio State University. "But if you cut a few trees in the middle, it won't reach your house."

That's the theory behind the transcranial magnetic stimulator, a hairdryer-sized device that creates a magnetic pulse that, when held against the back of a patient's head, interrupts the electrical activity during the aura, according to a study funded by the manufacturer, NeuraLieve. The firm is applying to the FDA for approval, says Mohammad, the study's lead author.

A Healthy Lifestyle Can Help

Mauskop, director of the New York Headache Center, believes most patients could control their migraines with over-the-counter medications and "headache hygiene," including sleeping, eating and exercising regularly.

Mohammad agrees. "Healthy lifestyle—exercise, yoga, hydration to alleviate tension—is important because we know stress can trigger an attack," he says.

Safer has tried her share of alternative treatments, including feverfew (a plant in the sunflower family), acupuncture, massage, hypnosis, magnesium injections, biofeedback, wearing a bite guard and listening to [German composer and musician Johann Sebastian] Bach. "I offer myself for any treatment that doesn't involve cutting off my head," she says.

She encourages other patients to see a doctor and "be activists in their treatments."

> **FAST FACT**
>
> The term *migraine* is derived from the Greek word *hemikrania*, meaning "half of the head."

New Drugs Are Not Always the Best Choice for Migraine Sufferers

Kerri Wachter

In the following viewpoint health writer Kerri Wachter maintains that newer drugs are not any better at preventing migraines than the older Food and Drug Administration–approved drugs are. Double-blind studies reveal that the newer drug topiramate has about the same level of effectiveness as several currently prescribed drugs do. Moreover, topiramate has a few potentially serious side effects, and it is far more expensive than the older drugs. The most useful tool in treating chronic migraine, Wachter notes, is teaching patients how to monitor their doses and avoid migraines that are triggered by medication overuse. Wachter is a senior writer for *Internal Medicine News*.

N ewer drugs aren't any better for migraine prophylaxis [prevention] than are older treatments and may be worse choices for many patients when cost is a factor.

SOURCE: Kerri Wachter, "Newer Drugs No Better for Migraine Prophylaxis," *Internal Medicine News*, August 1, 2008, p. 13. Reprinted by permission.

"There's no proof of increased efficacy with the newer drugs," said Dr. Gretchen E. Tietjen, chair of the department of neurology at the University of Toledo (Ohio).

Topiramate (Topamax), a newer drug, has been compared with several other drugs in head-to-head, double-blind studies, including divalproex sodium, nadolol, propranolol, and amitriptyline, she said at the annual meeting of the American College of Physicians. "In these head-to-head studies, there was similar efficacy."

Propranolol probably is the best-studied agent for migraine prevention and is Food and Drug Administration [FDA]–approved for that indication. "There are—so far—no other drugs that have been shown to have better efficacy," Dr. Tietjen said. However, because many of her patients have depression or asthma, two relative contraindications to using the drug, she prescribes it infrequently.

Open-label studies have suggested that, in patients who did not respond to propranolol alone or topiramate alone, the combination might be more effective, but more research is needed.

Side Effects and Cost

It's also important to consider potential side effects, Dr. Tietjen said. While topiramate doses of up to 100 mg are well tolerated, its uncommon but potentially serious side effects include paresthesias [tingling, prickling sensation] of the extremities, loss of appetite, depression, and confusion.

Cost also is a consideration. In her own informal survey of a local pharmacy, the monthly cost of the typical dosage of amitriptyline was $10, propranolol was $53, divalproex sodium was $128, and topiramate was $235. "So there's really a difference [in cost], especially when you don't see much difference in efficacy," Dr. Tietjen said.

> **FAST FACT**
>
> Potential side effects of the migraine drug topiramate include: slowed reflexes, foggy headedness, poor coordination, dizziness, memory loss, and double vision.

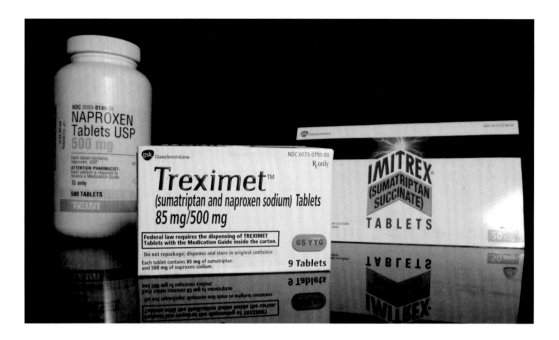

GlaxoSmithKline's new migraine medicine Treximet has been criticized by doctors and insurers alike for being no more effective in treating migraines than the older generic drugs it combines. (JB Reed/Bloomberg via Getty Images)

In a 2000 evidence-based review by the U.S. Headache Consortium—composed of several specialty societies—group I drugs were considered to have medium to high efficacy with good strength of evidence and mild to moderate side effects. These included amitriptyline, propanolol, timolol, and divalproex sodium. All but amitriptyline are FDA approved for migraine.

Group II medications either had lower efficacy or limited strength of evidence. This group included several [beta]-blockers (nadolol, metoprolol, atenolol), calcium-channel blockers (verapamil, nifedipine), an anticonvulsant (gabapentin), nonsteroidal anti-inflammatory drugs (naproxen sodium), magnesium, and vitamin B. (Topiramate had not been approved when this review was published.)

Medication Overuse or Analgesic Rebound Headache

The International Headache Society's most recent criteria for medication overuse headache include a headache present for more than 15 days/month, regular use for at least 3 months of one or more drugs that can be taken for acute and/or symptomatic treatment of headache, and a headache that has developed or markedly worsened during medication use.

Educating patients about the potential for developing medication overuse headaches and monitoring their medications are probably the most useful tools in treating these chronic headaches, Dr. Tietjen said.

Discontinuation of the use of abortive medications is the key to treatment. "For somebody you suspect of medication overuse headache . . . you want to stop the medication they're using. Whether you do it gradually or abruptly depends on the medication and depends on the patient," she said.

She also recommended starting the patient on a prophylactic medication. A number of transition regimens have been suggested, though these have not been well studied. Dr. Tietjen often uses dihy-droergotamine 0.5–1 mg every 8 hours for 2–3 days. This is a particularly good option for hospital inpatients who are stopping opioids and butalbital [drugs that can be prescribed for relief of headache pain], she said. . . .

Oral Contraceptives for Hormonal Migraine Headaches

Hormonal headaches include pure menstrual headaches and those related to the menstrual cycle. Pure menstrual migraines occur in a consistent relationship with menstruation and do not occur at other times of the month. It's estimated that about 15% of women with migraine have the pure menstrual variety. Menstruation-related migraines occur not only in a consistent relationship with menstruation but also at other times of the month.

An estimated 60% of women migraineurs [people having migraines] have this type.

"Studies have really strongly suggested that menstrual migraines are generally more severe, more intractable to therapy, [and] usually have more associated symptoms, like nausea and sensitivity to light and sound," Dr. Tietjen said.

In studies that have looked at low-dose (3–35 mcg [micrograms] ethinyl estradiol) oral contraceptives for the treatment of menstrual headaches, half to two-thirds of women reported no change, a quarter to a third reported migraine worsening, and only about 10% reported improvement.

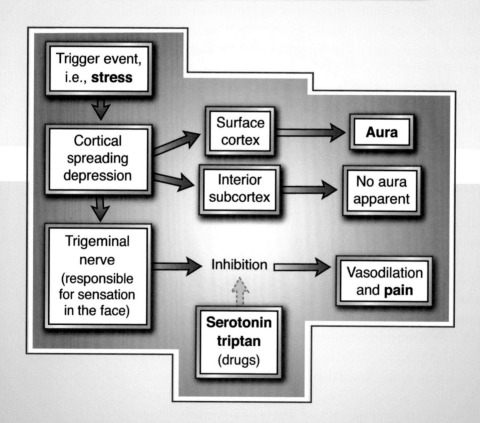

A Model of the Migraine Mechanism

Trigger event, i.e., **stress**

Cortical spreading depression

Surface cortex → **Aura**

Interior subcortex → No aura apparent

Trigeminal nerve (responsible for sensation in the face) → Inhibition → Vasodilation and **pain**

Serotonin triptan (drugs)

Taken from: Craig Blackwell, "Recent Model of Migraine Mechanism," www.blackwelleyesight.com.

Triptans appear to be effective for both menstrual and nonmenstrual headaches. Analgesics [pain relievers], such as naproxen sodium, also appear to be effective.

Several studies have looked at triptans for short-term prevention of predictable menstrual headaches. Naratriptan 1 mg or frovatriptan 2.5 mg administered twice daily for 6 days/month have been shown to be effective and well tolerated.

Both the World Health Organization and the American College of Obstetricians and Gynecologists have published consensus guidelines addressing migraine. Both recommend that women with migraine who are older than 35 years generally should not use oral contraceptives nor should women of any age with migraine with aura.

In general, Dr. Tietjen does not use oral contraceptives to treat menstrual migraines. If a migraine patient wants to use oral contraceptives, she recommends a low-dose monophasic [unchanging dose] regimen.

Dr. Tietjen reported that she has received research support from Glaxo-SmithKline Inc. and NMT Medical Inc.

Most Migraine Sufferers Are Dissatisfied with Their Medications

PR Newswire

When five-hundred clinically diagnosed migraine patients were surveyed about their treatment, the majority of them expressed frustration with their current medication, reports PR Newswire in the following selection. Most of these research subjects say that their medicine does not work fast enough and that it fails to relieve every migraine attack. Given that more than 60 percent of migraine sufferers experience rapid-onset migraine accompanied by nausea and vomiting, medical researchers are recognizing the need for fast-acting, non-oral treatment options. PR Newswire is a news and information distribution service.

I f an average day begins as a hectic race to get the kids off to school and get to work on time, imagine starting that day with a migraine. For many of the nation's 30 million migraine sufferers whose lives are often turned upside down by their migraines, relief can't come soon enough. In a new survey released [in June 2010] by

SOURCE: PR Newswire, "New Survey Reveals Critical Demand for Fast Migraine Relief," June 7, 2010. Reprinted by permission.

the National Headache Foundation (NHF), 3 in 4 migraine sufferers said their current medication doesn't work fast enough to get them back to their life when a migraine strikes suddenly or upon waking. . . .

"Migraine knowledge and treatments have advanced exponentially over the last 40 years, but these new study findings are a reminder that we have only begun to scratch the surface of this complex, biological disease," said Robert Dalton, executive director, NHF. "More education, along with awareness and adoption of the newest treatment options, is critical for migraine sufferers who are not experiencing fast relief from their current medications." . . .

Key Survey Findings

In the national survey, 500 migraine sufferers were asked about their migraine attacks, treatment satisfaction and experiences, and desired prescription medication attributes:

- The majority of sufferers (54%) said their prescription oral migraine medication is not useful for every migraine attack, yet less than 20% use another prescribed medication when an oral tablet is not an option
- Nearly 1 in 4 who don't use another prescription medication simply endure their headaches

"It is critical that both physicians and patients communicate about the nature and impact of the migraines so they can choose the best treatment plan for them. Every migraine is not the same, so a single treatment approach may not work," said Roger Cady, M.D., vice president of the NHF board of directors, and director of the Headache Care Center in Springfield, MO. "Fast-acting, non-oral treatment options are needed particularly for those who experience migraine attacks associated with sudden onset, waking, nausea or vomiting."

In a 2010 survey by the National Headache Foundation, a majority of migraine sufferers reported that their oral migraine medication is not effective for every migraine attack. **(Lea Paterson/Photo Researchers, Inc.)**

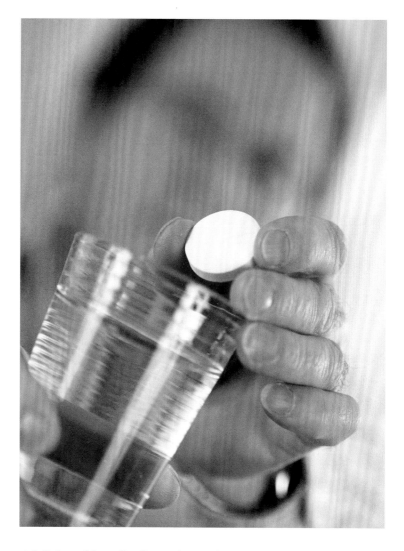

Additional key findings from the survey show that: *Sufferers aren't satisfied and highlight the need for speed in migraine relief.*

- A majority of sufferers (51%) are dissatisfied overall with their current medication.
- The most desired prescription medication attribute offered "the fastest relief possible regardless of form" (41%), followed by an "ability to use the medication and return to normal activities" (38%).

One treatment doesn't fit all migraine attacks.

- Rapid onset migraine was the most common type of attack, affecting 69% of respondents
- 66% also experience migraines with nausea and/or vomiting

Patient-physician dialogue isn't translating to better treatment.

- Most sufferers (roughly 2/3) have told their doctor that their prescription oral treatment doesn't work for all of their migraine attacks, yet only 1 in 4 say their doctor has told them they need more than one drug to manage their variable attacks.

"I have a stressful job, aging parents to check on, and nine grandchildren whom I love dearly. I am always on the go and don't have time for a migraine," said Sandie Griffin, 55, of Ozark, MO. "Fortunately, my doctor recently prescribed a new medication that quickly relieves my pain, and after years of literally losing days at a time to one headache, I have finally been liberated."

The Enormous Toll of Migraine

Migraine is a debilitating neurological condition characterized by throbbing pain, usually located on one side of the head and often accompanied by nausea and sensitivity to light and sound. Women are three times as likely as men to experience migraine. Poorly managed migraine translates to a potentially huge impact on a patient's quality of life—from missed or non-productive work days to lost family and personal time.

The direct and indirect costs associated with migraine are staggering: it is estimated that industry loses $31 billion per year due to absenteeism, lost productivity and medical expenses caused by migraine. Furthermore an estimated

> **FAST FACT**
>
> Some migraine sufferers experience pain relief after vomiting, but for others it signals the onset of the headache.

Side Effects of Commonly Prescribed Migraine Medicines

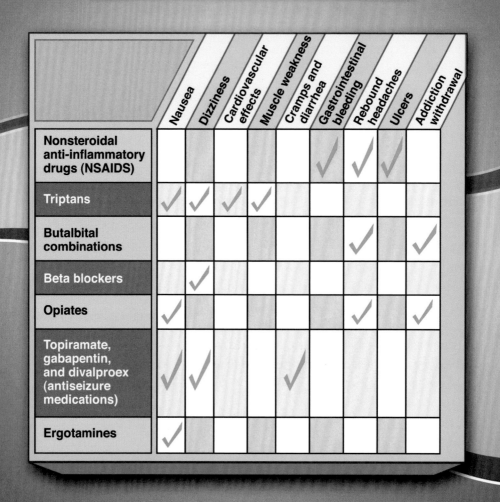

	Nausea	Dizziness	Cardiovascular effects	Muscle weakness	Cramps and diarrhea	Gastrointestinal bleeding	Rebound headaches	Ulcers	Addiction withdrawal
Nonsteroidal anti-inflammatory drugs (NSAIDS)						✓	✓	✓	
Triptans	✓	✓	✓	✓					
Butalbital combinations							✓		✓
Beta blockers		✓							
Opiates	✓						✓		✓
Topiramate, gabapentin, and divalproex (antiseizure medications)	✓	✓			✓				
Ergotamines	✓								

Taken from: WebMD. www.webmd.com.

157 million workdays are lost annually because of the pain and associated symptoms of migraine. The personal toll of migraine also is significant: in a recent study, nine out of 10 migraine sufferers reported they can't "function normally" during days in which a migraine strikes, and nearly three in 10 required bed rest. . . .

Survey Sponsors

The National Migraine Treatment Survey was conducted on behalf of the National Headache Foundation via telephone in March 2010. It included a national sample of 500 clinically diagnosed migraine sufferers between the ages of 25 and 45. The survey was supported by [pharmaceutical companies] Zogenix, Inc. and Astellas Pharma US, Inc.

The Outlook for Migraine Sufferers Has Greatly Improved

Barb Berggoetz

Migraine sufferers have often found that the drugs prescribed for their condition either work inconsistently or cause side effects. Furthermore, the most commonly prescribed class of drugs, triptans, are contraindicated for those with risk factors for cardiovascular disease, high cholesterol, or diabetes. However, several promising remedies are on the horizon, writes Barb Berggoetz in the following viewpoint. Certain newer drugs with fewer dangerous side effects offer the possibility of interfering with a developing migraine, while others work as preventives. Also, nondrug remedies, such as the use of neural stimulators that send electrical currents through the brain, can reverse or reduce migraine symptoms, she says. Many patients learn, through trial and error, that a combination of medications, nondrug therapies such as biofeedback and massage, and avoidance of known migraine triggers reduces the number of migraines they experience. Berggoetz is a health and fitness reporter for the *Indianapolis Star* newspaper.

SOURCE: Barb Berggoetz, "Heading Off the Pain of Migraines: For the Millions of Americans Suffering from Chronic Migraines, the Outlook for Relief Is Better than It's Been in Years," *Saturday Evening Post.* January/February 2009, pp. 50–53. Reprinted by permission.

Debra BenAvram's health woes kicked off with a "really horrible" migraine three years ago [in 2006]. She has no idea what triggered the attack. But over the next six months, it turned into a constant daily headache that forced her home from work each afternoon.

Since then, much of her life has been filled with a myriad of drugs and specialists, two surgeries to relieve neck and head nerve pressure, nausea, acupuncture, holistic diets, fatigue, days in bed. And lots of frustration. But she's persevered.

"I just haven't wanted to cave," said the 32-year-old CEO [chief executive officer] of a medical society in Silver Spring, Maryland, outside of Washington, D.C. "For me, I feel like it would be giving up. I have a son, a job I love and care about, and a family. I'm not ready to give up."

BenAvram has found some relief, though, thanks to the Diamond Headache Clinic in Chicago and more effective medications. She's down to 10 to 12 fewer severe migraines a month—cut by more than half. But like many of the more than 29 million Americans suffering migraines, she struggles to keep them under control with a combination of drugs, dietary changes, and other methods.

A Daily Challenge

It's a daily challenge for 10 percent of the population dealing with this painful and often debilitating headache disorder. More women—one in five—are affected than men (one in 20).

Yet the outlook for migraine sufferers is better than it's been in years.

Drug research and development for migraine and chronic headache treatments is escalating, with new medications and different forms of drug and nondrug treatments in the pipeline or close to the market.

Among them are skin patches, nasal powders, inhalation devices, a portable transcranial magnetic stimulator

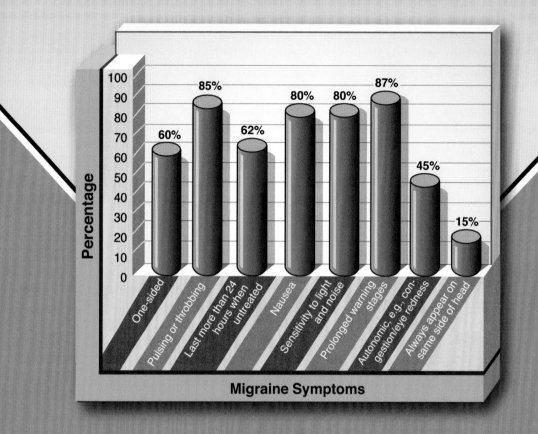

Migraine Statistics: Symptoms

Percentage vs. Migraine Symptoms

- One-sided: 60%
- Pulsing or throbbing: 85%
- Last more than 24 hours when untreated: 62%
- Nausea: 80%
- Sensitivity to light and noise: 80%
- Prolonged warning stages: 87%
- Autonomic; e.g.; congestion/eye redness: 45%
- Always appear on same side of head: 15%

Taken from: Randolph W. Evans, "A Review of Headache," August 2009. www.rwevansmd.com.

(TMS), a surgically implanted stimulator, and the first new class of drugs for migraine prevention in 15 years. Successful clinical trials for some of these new developments impressed experts at the annual American Headache Society's conference last June [2008] in Boston.

"It's a very exciting period of time for headache drugs. It's exciting because of the interest of drug manufacturers," said Dr. Seymour Diamond, cofounder of the National Headache Foundation and one of the pioneers in headache research. He opened the first private headache clinic in 1972 in Chicago.

More than 20 pharmaceutical and biotech companies are in the middle of research or developing drugs and other remedies to treat headaches and migraines. Seymour said the Food and Drug Administration's [FDA's] approval in 1992 of the first triptan, a drug specifically designed for the acute treatment of migraine, made the drug industry realize a financial market existed for drugs for the long-standing headache sufferer.

But the drug-approval process is a long, arduous one requiring, on average, 10 to 15 years to go from lab testing to the pharmacy. In the end, only one in five drugs tested on humans is approved for the market.

New Approaches Are Needed

The new potential remedies are coming none too soon for migraine sufferers.

Despite the development of the popular triptans, many migraine sufferers still aren't getting adequate treatment or the relief they need, according to the recent American Migraine Prevalence and Prevention Study, sponsored by the National Headache Foundation. It concluded physicians have not dramatically changed their approach to the treatment of migraine in the past 10 years.

"We know that less than half of the people (with migraines) are being treated for migraines at any one time," said Dr. Stephen Silberstein, neurology professor and director of the Jefferson Headache Center at Thomas Jefferson University in Philadelphia.

The drugs either don't work for them, cause side effects, or people are afraid to take them, experts say.

Triptans are the most often prescribed and most effective drugs in stopping a migraine attack after it begins, according to Silberstein. They work by stimulating serotonin, a neurotransmitter found in the brain, to reduce inflammation and constrict blood vessels. But people with a past history of, or risk factors for, heart disease, high blood pressure, high cholesterol, angina, stroke, or diabetes can't use them.

In the future, Silberstein expects more nondrug options, and more alternatives to injections will be available, both of which will make seeking treatment more appealing.

Potential Alternatives to the Common Triptans

The first new class of drugs since triptans for the acute treatment of migraines is awaiting FDA approval now and could be on the market by 2010, he said. A so-called receptor antagonist drug, telcagepant—developed by Merck & Company—blocks the effect of calcitonin gene–related peptide (CGRP) released from nerve endings during a migraine.

"It's as effective as a class of triptans, but it has no side effects and doesn't create cardiovascular effects," said Silberstein. "More people should be able to safety take it."

Another promising class of migraine prevention drugs essentially calms down the nerve or glial cells in the brain, he said. Research presented at the headache conference shows these cells talk to and regulate each other. During migraine attacks, abnormal activity occurs in these cells. The tablet drug, called tonabersat—developed by England-based Minster Pharmaceuticals—interferes with this process, stopping migraines from developing.

Nondrug Remedies

Future drugs, Diamond predicted, should be more effective because they will abort or reverse migraines, and some may actually prevent them, with fewer side effects. Some nondrug remedies may be particularly attractive because they don't involve any side effects.

One of those, nicknamed the "zapper," uses a portable electronic device about the size of a hairdryer to administer two painless magnetic pulses that "zap" the

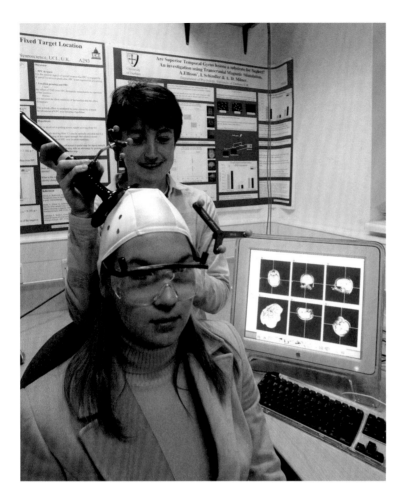

A woman undergoes transcranial magnetic stimulation. The treatment affects the aura phase that may precede migraines, in which people experience flashes of light, loss of vision, tingling, and confusion. (**Simon Fraser/University of Durham/Photo Researchers, Inc.**)

neurons in the brain. Called a transcranial magnetic stimulator (TMS), it affects the aura phase before migraines begin when people experience flashes or showers of light, loss of vision, and tingling or confusion: the device is also used for other purposes, such as treating severe depression.

The TMS works by sending a strong electric current through a metal coil, creating an intense magnetic field for about one millisecond. This magnetic pulse, when held against a person's head, generates an electric current in the neurons of the brain, interrupting the aura before it results in a throbbing headache.

"This is a landmark in the treatment of migraines," said Dr. Yousef M. Mohammad, a neurologist and assistant professor at Ohio State University, who is the principal investigator of a study at Ohio State's Medical Center that found the device safe and effective in eliminating headaches when used as they begin.

Last June [2008], Mohammad reported to the American Headache Society that of 164 patients involved in the multi-university, randomized clinical trial receiving TMS treatment, 39 percent were pain-free at the two-hour post-treatment point. That compares to 22 percent who were pain-free after receiving "sham" pulses—due to a placebo effect.

"Since almost all migraine drugs have some side effects, and patients are prone to addiction from narcotics or developing headaches from frequent use of over-the-counter medication, the TMS device holds great promise for migraine sufferers," said Mohammad.

If the FDA approves the device for migraines, he expects it to be on the market in about six months.

Preventive Medications

The device sounds worth trying to Patti Salinas, 43, a long-time migraine sufferer from Channahon, Illinois, south of Chicago. "If it's something that helps and prevents migraines, I would try anything."

Fortunately, she's already found some relief, even if not complete.

At age 10, she started having headaches. When she was in her mid-20s, the migraines became debilitating. She'd have four migraines a month, with milder headaches in between from taking lots of over-the-counter drugs.

Her migraines could last six to eight hours and literally put her out of action. "I could do nothing but lay down and put ice packs against my head in a dark room. No sound, no light, nothing that had a scent to it."

Salinas and other migraine sufferers say people who don't have migraines usually don't have a clue about how bad they can be.

"For me, it's a throbbing, severe pain in the back of my neck, and it feels like my brain is being squeezed," she said. "It can even affect your eye sockets so [that] you want to take your eyeballs out and massage them to take the pain away."

For many like Salinas, migraines interfere with their lives.

She had to leave her office job at a utility company when they'd hit. She couldn't drive. She'd also have to get childcare for her son. After Salinas relied on over-the-counter and sinus medication, a neurologist prescribed an analgesic with anti-inflammatory properties that helped for a couple years.

But the migraines persisted, so she sought help at the Diamond Clinic [in 2004]. She learned about headache triggers, kept a log of her headaches, took many tests, and stopped all over-the-counter drugs except ibuprofen. Preventive medications—daily dosages of Inderal and Vivactal—and Imitrex injections she does herself for a severe headache have helped limit her migraines to only one every couple months.

"I still get headaches, but now I know how to treat them," said Salinas. "I think it's manageable. My quality of life is better. The severity and frequency (of migraines) have decreased with these preventive drugs."

Other Options

For those with chronic, intractable migraines who can't find such relief, another type of stimulator may be the answer. A study presented at the recent headache conference showed promising results from occipital nerve stimulation (ONS), said Silberstein.

FAST FACT

A 2002 study conducted by neurologist Licia Grazzi and others found that the use of biofeedback in combination with medication is more successful than medication alone in treating migraines.

ONS treatment involves implanting a neurostimulator under the skin at the base of the head. The device delivers electrical impulses near the occipital nerves via insulated lead wires tunneled under the skin. People can adjust it themselves.

While the cost isn't estimated yet, he said the device may be federally approved and on the market within a couple years.

In addition to the potential new drugs and devices, migraine sufferers may get some additional choices with generic versions of existing medications, drugs being re-packaged into different modes of delivery, and new combinations of drugs.

Here are some of the options under study, according to the National Headache Foundation:

- Drugs previously used to treat conditions such as epilepsy, depression, and Alzheimer's may have an impact on headaches and migraines. Ongoing clinical trials involve Aricept, an Alzheimer's drug; Neurontin, an anti-convulsant; and others.
- A transdermal skin patch contains a drug and a small battery-powered electronic controller that precisely controls the rate and amount of drug released from the patch. A patch using zolmitriptan is in clinical trials.
- A nasal powder form of dihydroergotamine from Britannia Pharmaceuticals may be easier to use and more rapidly absorbed than the current nasal spray form.
- An inhalation device uses heat to vaporize a drug into an odorless mist that passes through the lungs into the bloodstream, perhaps providing relief within 60 seconds. The Staccato device from Alexza Molecular Delivery Corp. is in clinical trials using prochlorperazine.
- Oral and intranasal generic sumatriptan are expected to be available in 2009.

Ashley Etters's Story

Even with all the promise of new drug and nondrug therapies, experts advise those who experience chronic headaches and migraines to find out and avoid the triggers in their environment and diets that prompt an attack.

A migraine sufferer since age 4, Ashley Etters of Cary, Illinois, has to stay clear of many different foods and scents—caffeine, chocolate, candles, perfumes. Etters, now a 19-year-old Illinois State University student, knows to avoid extended time in the sun and going without eating for too long.

Unfortunately, she's learned this through years of experience with migraines, causing her to miss a lot of school and interfering with basketball and soccer practices.

"I usually got them for 48 to 72 hours. I was always throwing up with them. I had to sleep in a dark, quiet room or just lay there," she recalled. "It felt like someone was taking a hammer to my head."

Now Etters, who takes preventive medications every day, gets a bad migraine about once a month as well as various minor headaches that she's able to control all the time.

"I don't think I'm ever going to get rid of them," she said, seeming resigned to put up with them, as her mother has done for 25 years. Still, she knows how to adapt by taking steps like not falling behind in her studies. If she did, stress would lead to an inevitable migraine.

Regulating Stress

Stress can also be relieved by other strategies, such as good exercise and massages, and nondrug therapy like biofeedback, say headache experts.

"It's not a cure-all, but it can work prophylactically [preventively] in many people because stress is one of the triggers of headaches," said Diamond, who studied using biofeedback for migraines more than 30 years ago.

Biofeedback is a method that teaches people to control bodily functions such as heart rate, blood pressure, and muscle tension, which were once considered to be beyond voluntary control. Research has shown that by monitoring these functions and feeding back information to people on an ongoing and immediate basis, through visual and auditory instruments, voluntary control can actually be taught.

Using techniques of self-regulation, people can learn to change specific responses of the body, such as releasing muscle tension and spasm, lowering blood pressure, and diminishing headache pain.

No matter what combination of drugs and nondrug therapies they're using, migraine sufferers often have to stay on high alert—avoiding known triggers but also worrying about attacks they can't control.

After years of not being able to make definite plans, BenAvram's life is getting somewhat more predictable. She has responded better to the beta-blocker, antiinflammatory and antinausea medications she takes. She also knows what to do and not do, eat and not eat.

"You have to wake up at the same time every day," she said. "I have to eat lunch at noon or I'm going to have a headache at 12:30. I haven't had alcohol in three years."

Still, her migraines force her to leave work sometimes. Her scalp is so sensitive, she can't wear hats, headbands, or tight sunglasses. Her doctor at the Diamond Clinic thinks she'll always be a headache patient.

"But it's definitely better," she said optimistically. "I just try to tell myself, 'This is a good month or this was not a good month.' I've had two good months in a row. That's more than I've had in the last two years."

Traditional Chinese Medicine Offers Effective Therapies for Migraine Sufferers

Harry Hong

Harry Hong is a biochemist and a doctor of traditional Chinese medicine (TCM) stationed in Hoffman Estates, Illinois. In the following essay Hong outlines a traditional Chinese approach to treating migraine, which includes taking a thorough diagnostic history of the patient, applying acupuncture, and prescribing medicinal herbs and dietary restrictions. Hong maintains that migraine is rooted in disharmonies and deficiencies within various body systems, an imbalance between yin and yang energies, and pathogenic factors, such as wind, damp, heat, and cold. TCM, as well as physical exercise and mind-calming techniques, restore balance to the body, thereby relieving and preventing migraine attacks.

Migraine headache is a recurrent neurovascular headache disorder characterized by attacks of debilitating pain associated with photophobia, phonophobia, and nausea and vomiting. The highest incidence of migraine occurs between the ages of 20 and 35

SOURCE: Harry Hong, "Migraine Headache and Traditional Chinese Medicine," www.harryhong.com. The Healing Light Company, 2009. Reprinted by permission.

and is often associated with a positive family history of the disease. Migraine headaches are classified into two diagnostic categories: migraine with and without aura. Migraine without aura (common migraine) consists of unilateral or generalized cephalgia [head pain], throbbing or pulsatile in nature, in conjunction with nausea, vomiting, and photophobia. Migraine with aura is preceded by a 15–20 minute episode of visual or sensory aura. Auras are most likely visual alterations, usually experienced as hemianopsia and scotomata [diminished field of vision] that enlarge and spread peripherally.

Traditional Chinese Medicine

From the viewpoint of traditional Chinese medicine (TCM), migraine headaches are classified according to the overall condition of the patient, not only the nature of the headache. The headache is a result of disturbance or imbalance of *Yin-Yang* within the *Zang-Fu* organ system or the Channel system (Meridians), which are the two principal systems that regulate the functions of the body and mind. The diagnosis of TCM is the unique pattern differentiation of the clinical symptom-complexes, which represent specific pathological conditions that can be adjusted or reversed to physiological conditions by TCM therapeutic techniques such as medicinal herbs, acupuncture and *Qi Gong* therapy.

The disharmony of the Liver system is the most common reason causing migraine headache. According to the Zang-Fu theory, the Liver is the organ system that regulates the flow of *Qi* [energy] as well as stores the soul (related to mental activity). The smooth flow of Qi regulates emotional activities as well as ensures that the overall body activity operates normally. The disharmony of the Liver system, most commonly deficiency of Yin energy or excess of Yang energy, causes irregular Qi flow and Blood stasis, and accumulates Heat inside the body. Both the Qi stagnation and the Heat accumulation may result in migraine headache. The Liver type of migraine shows moderate to severe intensity, sometimes with pulsating quality and aggravation by walking stairs or physical exercise. This type of migraine is commonly in conjunction with emotional strain or stress, feeling of oppression in the chest and hypochondrium, depression or anxiety, reddened tongue with thin coating, and taut pulse.

Deficiency of the Kidneys is another common reason to cause migraine, especially for those patients with a long history of headache. According to the theory of the Five Elements (Phases), Water (Kidney) energy produces Wood (Liver) energy. The Kidney deficiency, caused by prolonged illness, may result in the Liver Yin deficiency and trigger headache. The Kidney deficient type of migraine shows mild to moderate intensity and is commonly in conjunction with weakness of lower back, low energy, lassitude, pale tongue, deep and weak pulse. Clinically there is a third type of migraine, which is the combination of the Liver type and the Kidney type of headache. The Liver Qi stagnation and Kidney deficiency may co-exist in the same patient.

> **FAST FACT**
>
> The US National Institutes of Health report that acupuncture is an acceptable alternative treatment that can be included as part of a migraine pain management program.

Migraine headaches are also triggered by other pathogenic factors such as Wind, Damp, Heat and Cold. Examining the nature of the headache usually helps to identify the factors causing the headache. For example, Wind causes a moving headache (the location of the pain changes); Damp results in a headache with heaviness; Cold causes a headache that may get worse when the temperature drops. In addition, the location of the headache also makes a difference. The forehead headache is usually related to Stomach meridian, the crown and back headache is related to Bladder meridian, while the side headache is usually related to the Liver or Gall Bladder meridian. However, the major pathophysiological change of the body is the Qi stagnation and Blood stasis.

Pattern differentiation process recognizes the signature symptoms for each organ system as well as the pathogenic factors. Proper diagnosis should be made through analyzing the complete history of the patients and all presenting symptoms, followed by checking the tongue and taking pulse.

Conventional Western Medicine Versus Traditional Chinese Medicine

Currently no cure exists for migraine with allopathic [mainstream] medicine, although some degree of control can be achieved using symptomatic therapy, including simple analgesics [pain relievers], nonsteroidal anti-inflammatory drugs (NSAIDs), ergot derivatives, dihydroergotamine, serotonin agonists, and even corticosteroids or opioid analgesics. Because of the possible side effect of the drugs for migraine, more and more people have started to search for alternatives. TCM approaches to solving migraine focus on the imbalance of the whole body, which is the common reason causing headache. TCM therapies, a combination of Chinese herbs, acupuncture, manipulation, and Qi Gong therapy, are often more specific to each patient's condition according to their specific diagnostic categories.

Acupuncture is the most common therapy for migraine. Efficacy of acupuncture towards migraine headache has been reported by many independent studies. Clinical trials showed significant decrease in the number of headaches and their duration after acupuncture treatment. The attacks were less severe and drug intake was reduced and did not re-increase until follow-ups. Acupuncture analgesia has been thoroughly studied since the 70s. The major finding through these studies indicated that acupuncture stimulates endogenous morphine-like molecules such as endorphin and monoamine to block the pain signal. But acupuncture does far more than just the pain relief. It modulates endocrine and nervous system and stimulates self-healing process of the body. The actual mechanism is still unknown.

Acupuncture therapy uses very thin needles to stimulate acupuncture points on the skin. For migraine headache the following acupuncture points are commonly used: *Hegu* (LI 4), *Tainchong* (Lv 3), *Zulinqi* (GB), and *Fengchi* (GB), etc. From my experience, a non-invasive electroacupuncture is also useful for this condition. Electroacupuncture is a method of stimulating acupuncture points with mild electric current. A number of points along the Stomach and Gall Bladder meridian on shoulder, neck and head, are often used. Electroacupuncture effectively relieves headache and relaxes tension of the muscle around the neck and shoulder. Chinese *Tui Na* (manipulation) for the neck and back also helps to relieve the headache. Dosage, duration and frequency of the

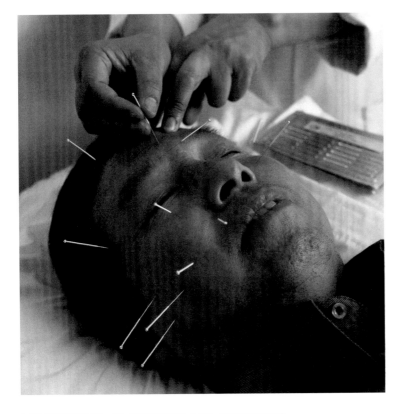

An acupuncturist inserts needles into a man's head and face. Acupuncture is the most common alternative treatment for migraines.
(Tex Image/Photo Researchers, Inc.)

therapy depend on individual patient. Most patients get some degree of relief after a single treatment. But the pain may come back after a few hours to a couple of days. This is due to the imbalance of the body. Multiple treatment is highly recommended because acupuncture analgesia has

Acupoint 7 for Migraine

An acupoint is any of the various places on the body where pressure is applied in acupressure treatments or in which a needle is inserted during acupuncture, often resulting in relief of symptoms.

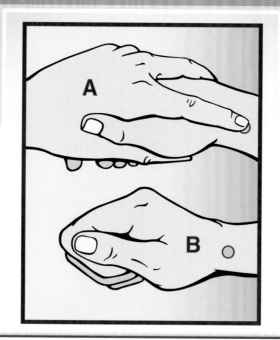

Clasp your hands together (A), touching your upper wrist with your forefinger. The acupoint is found on a line with the thumb, in a small depression (B); remembering the position of the point, unclasp hands and apply pressure.

Taken from: Kevin T. Boyd, "PointFinder: the Online Acupressure Guide," http://med.stanford.edu/personal/pointfinder/#findingpoints.

proven to be accumulative. Normally twice a week for 4–6 weeks (8–12 visits) is recommended. Complex cases with severe imbalance of the body may need longer time. For most of the cases, a properly prescribed Chinese herbal formula helps the patient to recover faster.

Herbal Medicine Is at the Center of Treatment

Chinese herbal medicine is another common therapy for migraine headache. Chinese herbal medicine has been used to balance the body with natural products for thousands of years. The theory behind Chinese herbs is the unique Yin-Yang and Zang-Fu theory, which is parallel to Western physiology. For the disharmony of the Liver system, the principle of treatment is to smooth the flow of Liver Qi and clear the Liver Heat. The prescription is based on specific symptoms of each patient as well as the experience of each practitioner. Decoction of Bupleurum chinensis (*Chai Hu*), Angelica sinensis (*Dang Gui*) and Paeonia lactiflora (*Bai Shao*) in combination with other herbs is commonly used. For the pattern of Kidney deficiency, the principle of treatment is to reinforce vital energy of the Kidney and Liver. The prescription is usually the decoction of Rehmannia gutinosa (*Di Huang*), Dioscorea opposita (*Shan Yao*) and Comus officinalis (*Shan Yu Rou*) with modifications. Patent formula is also available for both cases. Chinese herbal medicine is the core of traditional Chinese therapies for migraine headache and is very powerful to balance the body. It significantly reduces the pain, shortens the headache attacking time, reduces the frequency of the migraine and prevents the headache from happening. The duration of Chinese herbal treatment is usually 1–2 months and also depends on individual patient's condition.

The tense lifestyle in the modern society is one of the reasons causing migraine headache and other related illness. The regularity of lifestyle, such as eating, resting and sleeping, is important for migraine patients in addition to the herbal and acupuncture treatment. Regular physical exercise, emotional control techniques and other calm activities are also necessary to prevent migraine attacking. Qi Gong is an ancient Chinese technique to actively promote circulation of Qi in the body and adjust the body inner clock to the natural clock. Similar to Yoga meditation, Qi Gong is the Chinese way to control and cultivate the energy of our body. It also serves as emotional control technique to prevent migraine headaches. *Tai Ji Quan* is another popular exercise in Chinese society. It combines Qi Gong and physical exercise and allows people to practice regularly to relax and adjust the conflict among the organ systems caused by the modern lifestyle. Both Qi Gong and Tai Ji Quan can be very good self-help techniques for migraine.

Diet Can Balance the Body

Diet is considered an important influence of health and illness in TCM. Food is believed to be part of the medicine and affects the result of the herbal treatment. According to Chinese theory, food is classified into different groups according to their nature and taste. Fatty and greasy foods, alcohol, coffee or sweets can produce Dampness and Heat, while spicy also produces Heat. Migraine patients should avoid those food items in their diet, especially for those patients diagnosed with the disharmony of the Liver. On the other hand, diet is believed to complement the nature of each human body. Properly designed diet plan according to Chinese theories will compensate Yin-Yang nature of the body and benefit the overall health in a long run. Consult a TCM practitioner for more information about the diet of each specific case.

The Effectiveness of Traditional Chinese Medicine Has Not Been Proved

Stephen Barrett

Claims that traditional Chinese medicine (TCM) offers consistently effective treatments for chronic conditions are dubious, writes Stephen Barrett in the following selection. While one form of TCM—acupuncture—can relieve pain, it does so unpredictably for most people and not at all for some people, Barrett states. Studies show that many people respond to fake (nonpenetrating) acupuncture needles, which suggests that acupuncture's pain-reducing qualities may be simply the result of mental suggestion, cultural conditioning, or the placebo effect. The practice of acupuncture and other forms of TCM are based on primitive concepts of illness that cannot stand up to present-day science, the author concludes. Barrett, a retired psychiatrist, is the head of *Quackwatch*, an international network of people who are concerned about health-related frauds, myths, fads, and fallacies.

SOURCE: Stephen Barrett, "Be Wary of Acupuncture, Qigong, and 'Chinese Medicine,'" *Quackwatch*, December 30, 2007. Reprinted by permission.

"Chinese medicine," often called "Oriental medicine" or "traditional Chinese medicine (TCM)," encompasses a vast array of folk medical practices based on mysticism. It holds that the body's vital energy (*chi* or *qi*) circulates through channels, called *meridians,* that have branches connected to bodily organs and functions. Illness is attributed to imbalance or interruption of chi. Ancient practices such as acupuncture, *Qigong,* and the use of various herbs are claimed to restore balance.

Traditional Approaches

Traditional acupuncture, as now practiced, involves the insertion of stainless steel needles into various body areas. A low-frequency current may be applied to the needles to produce greater stimulation. Other procedures used separately or together with acupuncture include: moxibustion (burning of floss or herbs applied to the skin); injection of sterile water, procaine, morphine, vitamins, or homeopathic solutions through the inserted needles; applications of laser beams (laserpuncture); placement of needles in the external ear (auriculotherapy); and acupressure (use of manual pressure). Treatment is applied to "acupuncture points," which are said to be located throughout the body. Originally there were 365 such points, corresponding to the days of the year, but the number identified by proponents during the past 2,000 years has increased gradually to about 2,000.[1] Some practitioners place needles at or near the site of disease, whereas others select points on the basis of symptoms. In traditional acupuncture, a combination of points is usually used.

Qigong is also claimed to influence the flow of "vital energy." Internal Qigong involves deep breathing, concentration, and relaxation techniques used by individuals for themselves. External Qigong is performed by "Qigong masters" who claim to cure a wide variety of diseases with energy released from their fingertips. However, scientific investigators of Qigong masters in China have found no evidence of paranormal powers and some evidence of deception. They found, for example, that a patient lying on a table about eight feet from a Qigong master moved rhythmically or thrashed about as the master moved his hands. But when she was placed so that she could no longer see him, her movements were unrelated to his.[2] *Falun gong,* which China banned several years ago, is a Qigong variant claimed to be "a powerful mechanism for healing, stress relief and health improvements."

Most acupuncturists espouse the traditional Chinese view of health and disease and consider acupuncture, herbal medicine, and related practices to be valid approaches to the full gamut of disease. Others reject the traditional approach and merely claim that acupuncture offers a simple way to achieve pain relief. The diagnostic process used by TCM practitioners may include questioning (medical history, lifestyle), observations (skin, tongue, color), listening (breathing sounds), and pulse-taking. Six pulse aspects said to correlate with body organs or functions are checked on each wrist to determine which meridians are "deficient" in chi. (Medical science recognizes only one pulse, corresponding to the heartbeat, which can be felt in the wrist, neck, feet, and various other places.) Some acupuncturists state that the electrical properties of the body may become imbalanced weeks or even months before symptoms occur. These practitioners claim that acupuncture can be used to treat conditions when the patient just "doesn't feel right," even though no disease is apparent.

TCM (as well as the folk medical practices of various other Asian countries) is a threat to certain animal species. For example, black bears—valued for their gall bladders—have been hunted nearly to extinction in Asia, and poaching of black bears is a serious problem in North America.

Dubious Claims

The conditions claimed to respond to acupuncture include chronic pain (neck and back pain, migraine headaches), acute injury-related pain (strains, muscle and ligament tears), gastrointestinal problems (indigestion, ulcers, constipation, diarrhea), cardiovascular conditions (high and low blood pressure), genitourinary problems (menstrual irregularity, frigidity, impotence), muscle and nerve conditions (paralysis, deafness), and behavioral problems (overeating, drug dependence, smoking). However, the evidence supporting these claims consists mostly of practitioners' observations and poorly designed studies. A controlled study found that electroacupuncture of the ear was no more effective than placebo stimulation (light touching) against chronic pain.[3] In 1990, three Dutch epidemiologists analyzed 51 controlled studies of acupuncture for chronic pain and concluded that "the quality of even the better studies proved to be mediocre. . . . The efficacy of acupuncture in the treatment of chronic pain remains doubtful."[4] They also examined reports of acupuncture used to treat addictions to cigarettes, heroin, and alcohol, and concluded that claims that acupuncture is effective as a therapy for these conditions are not supported by sound clinical research.[5]

Acupuncture anesthesia is not used for surgery in the Orient to the extent that its proponents suggest. In China physicians screen out patients who appear to be unsuitable. Acupuncture is not used for emergency surgery and often is accompanied by local anesthesia or narcotic medication.[6]

How acupuncture may relieve pain is unclear. One theory suggests that pain impulses are blocked from reaching the spinal cord or brain at various "gates" to these areas. Another theory suggests that acupuncture stimulates the body to produce narcotic-like substances called *endorphins*, which reduce pain. Other theories suggest that the placebo effect, external suggestion (hypnosis), and cultural conditioning are important factors. [scientists Ronald] Melzack and [Patrick D.] Wall note that pain relief produced by acupuncture can also be produced by many other types of sensory hyperstimulation, such as electricity and heat at acupuncture points and elsewhere in the body. They conclude that "the effectiveness of all of these forms of stimulation indicates that acupuncture is not a magical procedure but only one of many ways to produce analgesia [pain relief] by an intense sensory input." In 1981, the American Medical Association Council on Scientific Affairs noted that pain relief does not occur consistently or reproducibly in most people and does not operate at all in some people.[7]

In 1995, George A. Ulett, M.D., Ph.D., Clinical Professor of Psychiatry, University of Missouri School of Medicine, stated that "devoid of metaphysical thinking, acupuncture becomes a rather simple technique that can be useful as a nondrug method of pain control." He believes that the traditional Chinese variety is primarily a placebo treatment, but electrical stimulation of about 80 acupuncture points has been proven useful for pain control.[8]

The quality of TCM research in China has been extremely poor. A 1999 analysis of 2,938 reports of clinical trials reported in Chinese medical journals concluded that that no conclusions could be drawn from the vast majority of them. The researchers stated:

> In most of the trials, disease was defined and diagnosed according to conventional medicine; trial outcomes were assessed with objective or subjective (or both) methods of conventional medicine, often complemented by traditional Chinese methods. Over 90% of the trials in non-specialist journals evaluated herbal treatments that were mostly proprietary Chinese medicines. . . . Although methodological quality has been improving over the years, many problems remain. The method of randomisation was often inappropriately described. Blinding

was used in only 15% of trials. Only a few studies had sample sizes of 300 subjects or more. Many trials used as a control another Chinese medicine treatment whose effectiveness had often not been evaluated by randomised controlled trials. Most trials focused on short term or intermediate rather than long term outcomes. Most trials did not report data on compliance and completeness of follow up. Effectiveness was rarely quantitatively expressed and reported. Intention to treat analysis was never mentioned. Over half did not report data on baseline characteristics or on side effects. Many trials were published as short reports. Most trials claimed that the tested treatments were effective, indicating that publication bias may be common; a funnel plot of the 49 trials of acupuncture in the treatment of stroke confirmed selective publication of positive trials in the area, suggesting that acupuncture may not be more effective than the control treatments.[9]

Two scientists at the University of Heidelberg have developed a "fake needle" that may enable acupuncture researchers to perform better-designed controlled studies. The device is a needle with a blunt tip that moves freely within a copper handle. When the tip touches the skin, the patient feels a sensation similar to that of an acupuncture needle. At the same time, the visible part of the needle moves inside the handle so it appears to shorten as though penetrating the skin. When the device was tested on volunteers, none suspected that it had not penetrated the skin.[10]

In 2004, a University of Heidelberg team proved the worth of their "sham acupuncture" technique in a study of postoperative nausea and vomiting (PONV) in women who underwent breast or gynecologic surgery. The study involved 220 women who received either acupuncture or the sham procedure at the acupuncture point "Pericardium 6" on the inside of the forearm. No significant difference in PONV or antivomiting medication use was found between the two groups or between the people who received treatment before anesthesia was induced and those who received it while anesthetized.[11] A subgroup analysis found that vomiting was "significantly reduced" among the acupuncture patients, but the authors correctly noted that this finding might be due to studying multiple outcomes. (As the number of different outcome measures increases, so do the odds that a "statistically significant" finding will be spurious.) This study is important because PONV reduction is one of the few alleged benefits of acupuncture supported by reports in scientific journals. However, the other positive studies were not as tightly controlled.

Harriet Hall, a retired family practitioner who is interested in quackery, has summed up the significance of acupuncture research in an interesting way:

> Acupuncture studies have shown that it makes no difference where you put the needles. Or whether you use needles or just pretend to use needles (as long as the subject believes you used them). Many acupuncture researchers are doing what I call Tooth Fairy science: measuring how much money is left under the pillow without bothering to ask if the Tooth Fairy is real.

Risks Exist

Improperly performed acupuncture can cause fainting, local hematoma (due to bleeding from a punctured blood vessel), pneumothorax (punctured lung), convulsions, local infections, hepatitis B (from unsterile needles), bacterial endocarditis, contact dermatitis, and nerve damage. The herbs used by acupuncture practitioners are not regulated for safety, potency, or effectiveness. There is also risk that an acupuncturist whose approach to diagnosis is not based on scientific concepts will fail to diagnose a dangerous condition.

The adverse effects of acupuncture are probably related to the nature of the practitioner's training. A survey of 1,135 Norwegian physicians revealed 66 cases of infection, 25 cases of punctured lung, 31 cases of increased pain, and 80 other cases with complications. A parallel survey of 197 acupuncturists, who are more apt to see immediate complications, yielded 132 cases of fainting, 26 cases of increased pain, 8 cases of pneumothorax, and 45 other adverse results.[12] However, a 5-year study involving 76 acupuncturists at a Japanese medical facility tabulated only 64 adverse event reports (including 16 forgotten needles and 13 cases of transient low blood pressure) associated with 55,591 acupuncture treatments. No serious complications were reported. The researchers concluded that serious adverse reactions are uncommon among acupuncturists who are medically trained.[13]

In 2001, members of the British Acupuncture Council who participated in two prospective studies reported low complication rates and no serious complications among patients who underwent a total of more than 66,000 treatments.[14,15] An accompanying editorial suggested that in competent hands, the likelihood of complications is small.[16] Since outcome data are not available, the studies cannot compare the balance of risks vs benefit. Nor do the studies take into account the likelihood of misdiagnosis (and failure to seek appropriate medical care) by practitioners who use traditional Chinese methods.

There is also financial risk. Online information suggests that the cost per visit ranges from about $50 to $100 per treatment, with the first visit to a practitioner costing more. Herbal products, which many practitioners commonly prescribe, could range anywhere from a few dollars to a few hundred dollars per month.

Questionable Standards

In 1971, an acupuncture boom occurred in the United States because of stories about visits to China by various

American dignitaries. Entrepreneurs, both medical and nonmedical, began using flamboyant advertising techniques to promote clinics, seminars, demonstrations, books, correspondence courses, and do-it-yourself kits. Today some states restrict the practice of acupuncture to physicians or others operating under their direct supervision. In about 20 states, people who lack medical training can perform acupuncture without medical supervision. The FDA now classifies acupuncture needles as Class II medical devices and requires labeling for one-time use by practitioners who are legally authorized to use them.[17] Acupuncture is not covered under Medicare. The March 1998 issue of the *Journal of the American Chiropractic Association* carried a five-part cover story encouraging chiropractors to get acupuncture training, which, according to one contributor, would enable them to broaden the scope of their practice.[18]

The National Certification Commission for Acupuncture and Oriental Medicine (NCCAOM) has set voluntary certification standards and offers separate certifications on Oriental medicine, acupuncture, Chinese herbology, and Asian bodywork therapy. In 2007, it reported that its certification programs or exams were . . . recognized for licensure in 40 states and the District of Columbia and that more than 20,000 practitioners are licensed in the United States.[19] (The Acupuncture. com Web site provides information on the licensing status of each state.) The credentials used by acupuncturists include C.A. (certified acupuncturist), Lic. Ac. (licensed acupuncturist), M.A. (master acupuncturist), Dip. Ac. (diplomate of acupuncture), Dipl.O.M. (diplomate of Oriental medicine), and O.M.D. (doctor of Oriental medicine). Some of these have legal significance, but they do not signify that the holder is competent to make adequate diagnoses or render appropriate treatment.

In 1990, the U.S. Secretary of Education recognized what is now called the Accreditation Commission for Acupuncture and Oriental Medicine (ACAOM) as an accrediting agency. However, such recognition is not based on the scientific validity of what is taught but upon other criteria.[20] Ulett has noted:

> Certification of acupuncturists is a sham. While a few of those so accredited are naive physicians, most are nonmedical persons who only play at being doctor and use this certification as an umbrella for a host of unproven New Age hokum treatments. Unfortunately, a few HMOs, hospitals, and even medical schools are succumbing to the bait and exposing patients to such bogus treatments when they need real medical care.

The National Council Against Health Fraud [NCAHF] has concluded:

- Acupuncture is an unproven modality of treatment.
- Its theory and practice are based on primitive and fanciful concepts of health and disease that bear no relationship to present scientific knowledge.
- Research during the past 20 years has not demonstrated that acupuncture is effective against any disease.
- Perceived effects of acupuncture are probably due to a combination of expectation, suggestion, counter-irritation, conditioning, and other psychologic mechanisms.
- The use of acupuncture should be restricted to appropriate research settings.
- Insurance companies should not be required by law to cover acupuncture treatment.
- Licensure of lay acupuncturists should be phased out.
- Consumers who wish to try acupuncture should discuss their situation with a knowledgeable physician who has no commercial interest.[21]

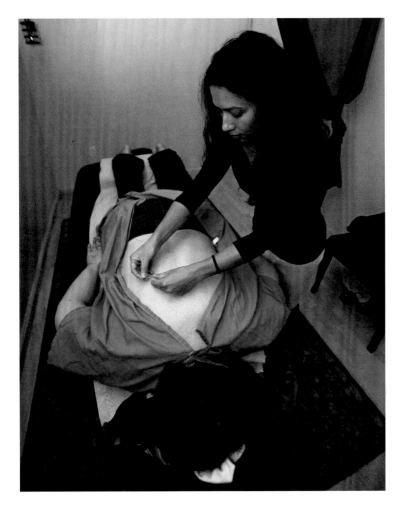

According to the National Council Against Health Fraud, the effectiveness of acupuncture as a treatment for migraines has not been proved. (**Lenny Ignelzi/AP Images**)

The NIH Debacle

In 1997, a Consensus Development Conference sponsored by the National Institutes of Health [NIH] and several other agencies concluded that "there is sufficient evidence . . . of acupuncture's value to expand its use into conventional medicine and to encourage further studies of its physiology and clinical value."[22] The panelists also suggested that the federal government and insurance companies expand coverage of acupuncture so more people can have access to it. These conclusions were not based on research done after NCAHF's position paper was published. Rather, they reflected the bias of the panelists who were selected by a planning committee dominated by acupuncture proponents.[23] NCAHF board chairman Wallace Sampson, M.D., has described the conference "a consensus of proponents, not a consensus of valid scientific opinion."

Although the report described some serious problems, it failed to place them into proper perspective. The panel acknowledged that "the vast majority of papers studying acupuncture consist of case reports, case series, or intervention studies with designs inadequate to assess efficacy" and that "relatively few" high-quality controlled trials have been published about acupuncture's effects. But it reported that "the World Health Organization has listed more than 40 [conditions] for which [acupuncture] may be indicated." This sentence should have been followed by a statement that the list was not valid.

Far more serious, although the consensus report touched on Chinese acupuncture theory, it failed to point out the danger and economic waste involved in going to practitioners who can't make appropriate diagnoses. The report noted:

- The general theory of acupuncture is based on the premise that there are patterns of energy flow (Qi) through the body that are essential for health. Disruptions of this flow are believed to be responsible for disease. The acupuncturist can correct imbalances of flow at identifiable points close to the skin.
- Acupuncture focuses on a holistic, energy-based approach to the patient rather than a disease-oriented diagnostic and treatment model.
- Despite considerable efforts to understand the anatomy and physiology of the "acupuncture points," the definition and characterization of these points remains controversial. Even more

FAST FACT

Researchers at Ruhr University Bochum in Germany say that the body may react positively to any thin needle prick—or that acupuncture may simply trigger a placebo effect.

elusive is the scientific basis of some of the key traditional Eastern medical concepts such as the circulation of Qi, the meridian system, and the five phases theory, which are difficult to reconcile with contemporary biomedical information but continue to play an important role in the evaluation of patients and the formulation of treatment in acupuncture.

Simply stated, this means that if you go to a practitioner who practices traditional Chinese medicine, you are unlikely to be properly diagnosed. Very few publications have mentioned this, which strikes me as very strange. Even *Consumer Reports* magazine has advised readers who want acupuncture treatment to consult a practitioner who is NCCAOM-certified. I advise people to avoid "certified" practitioners. Because the training needed for certification is based on nonsensical TCM theories, the safest way to obtain acupuncture is from a medical doctor who does research at a university-based medical school and does not espouse such theories.

Diagnostic Variability

In 1998, following a lecture I attended at a local college, an experienced TCM practitioner diagnosed me by taking my pulse and looking at my tongue. He stated that my pulse showed signs of "stress" and that my tongue indicated I was suffering from "congestion of the blood." A few minutes later, he told a woman that her pulse showed premature ventricular contractions (a disturbance of the heart's rhythm that could be harmless or significant, depending on whether the individual has underlying heart disease). He suggested that both of us undergo treatment with acupuncture and herbs—which would have cost about $90 per visit. I took the woman's pulse and found that it was completely normal. I believe that the majority of nonmedical acupuncturists rely on improper diagnostic procedures. The NIH consensus panel should have emphasized the seriousness of this problem.

Subsequent research has confirmed that TCM diagnosis has very little to do with people's real health problems. At least six studies have found that when multiple practitioners see the same patient, their TCM diagnoses vary considerably.

In a study published in 2001, a 40-year-old woman with chronic back pain who visited seven acupuncturists during a 2-week period was diagnosed with "Qi stagnation" by 6 of them, "blood stagnation" by 5, "kidney Qi deficiency" by 2, "yin deficiency" by 1, and "liver Qi deficiency" by 1. The proposed treatments varied even more. Among the six who recorded their recommendations, the practitioners planned to use between 7 and 26 needles inserted into 4 to 16 specific "acupuncture points" in the back, leg, hand, and foot. Of 28 acupuncture points selected, only 4 (14%) were prescribed by two or more acupuncturists.[24] The study appears to have been designed to make the results as consistent as possible. All of the acupuncturists had been trained at a school of traditional Chinese medicine (TCM). Six other volunteers were excluded because they "used highly atypical practices," and three were excluded because they had been in practice for less than three years. The study's authors stated that the diagnostic findings showed "considerable consistency" because nearly all of the practitioners found Qi or blood stagnation. However, the most likely explanation was that these are diagnosed in nearly everyone.

In another study, six TCM acupuncturists evaluated the same six patients on the same day. Twenty diagnoses and 65 acupoints were used at least once. The diagnosis of "Qi/Blood Stagnation with Kidney Deficiency" and the acupoint UB23 were used for every patient by most acupuncturists. However, consistency across acupuncturists regarding diagnostic details and other acupoints was poor. No diagnoses, and only one acupoint, were used preferentially for a subgroup of patients. Some diagnoses and treatment recommendations were dependent more on the practitioner than on the patient. Fine-grained diagnoses and most acupoints were unrelated to either patient or practitioner. The researchers concluded that TCM diagnoses and treatment recommendations for specific patients with chronic low back pain vary widely from one practitioner to another.[25]

Another study examined TCM diagnoses and treatments for patients with chronic low-back pain using two separate sets of treatment records. Information from more than 150 initial visits was available for analysis. A diagnosis of "Qi and Blood Stagnation" or "Qi Stagnation" was made for 85% of patients. A diagnosis of kidney deficiency (or one of its three subtypes) was made for 33%–51% of patients. Other specific diagnoses were made for less than 20% of the patients. An average of 12–13 needles was used in each treatment. Although more than 85 different acupoints were used in each data set, only 5 or 6 acupoints were used in more than 20 of the treatments in each data set. Only two of those acupoints (UB23, UB40) were the same for both sources of data. More than half of the patients received adjunctive treatments, including heat (36%–67%), and cupping (16%–21%). There was substantial variability in treatments among providers.[26]

In a larger study published in 2004, three TCM practitioners examined the same 39 rheumatoid arthritis (RA) patients separately at the University of Maryland General Clinical Research Center. Each patient filled out a questionnaire and underwent a physical examination that included tongue and pulse diagnosis. Then each practitioner provided both a TCM diagnosis and a herbal prescription. Agreement on TCM diagnoses among the 3 pairs of TCM practitioners ranged from 25.6% to 33.3%. The degree to which the herbal prescriptions agreed with textbook recommended practice of each TCM diagnosis ranged from 87.2% to 100%. The study's authors concluded:

> The total agreement on TCM diagnosis on RA patients among 3 TCM practitioners was low. When less stringent, but theoretically justifiable, criteria were employed, greater consensus was obtained. . . . The correspondence between the TCM diagnosis and the herbal formula prescribed for that diagnosis was high, although there was little agreement among the 3 practitioners with respect to the herbal formulas prescribed for individual patients.[27]

The University of Maryland researchers then repeated the above study using 40 RA patients and three practitioners who had had at least five years of experience. The results were nearly identical to the previous findings.[28]

In another study, 37 participants with frequent headaches were independently evaluated by three licensed acupuncturists said to be highly trained in TCM. The acupuncturists identified the meridians and type of dysfunction they believed were contributing to the participants' symptoms. The acupuncturists also ascribed one or more TCM diagnoses to each participant and selected eight acupuncture points for needling. Some variation in TCM pattern diagnosis and point selection was observed for all subjects. "Liver Yang" and "Qi dysfunction" were diagnosed in more than two thirds of subjects. Acupuncture points Liver 3, Large Intestine 4, and Governing Vessel (DU) 20 were the most commonly selected points for treatment.[29]

It would be fascinating to see what would happen if a healthy person who needed no medical treatment was examined by multiple acupuncturists.

The Bottom Line

TCM theory and practice are not based upon the body of knowledge related to health, disease, and health care that has been widely accepted by the scientific community. TCM practitioners disagree among themselves about how to diagnose patients and which treatments should go with which diagnoses. Even if they could agree, the TCM theories are so nebulous that no amount of scientific study will enable TCM to offer rational care.

For Additional Information
CSICOP Investigation of TCM and Pseudoscience in China
NCAHF Position Paper on Acupuncture
Questioning Dr. Isadore Rosenfeld's Acupuncture Story
Why TCM Diagnosis Is Worthless

References
1. Skrabanek P. Acupuncture: Past, present, and future. In Stalker D, Glymour C, editors. Examining Holistic Medicine. Amherst, NY: Prometheus Books, 1985.
2. Kurtz P, Alcock J, and others. Testing psi claims in China: Visit by a CSICOP delegation. Skeptical Inquirer 12:364–375, 1988.
3. Melzack R, Katz J. Auriculotherapy fails to relieve chronic pain: A controlled crossover study. JAMA 251:10411043, 1984.
4. Ter Reit G, Kleijnen J, Knipschild P. Acupuncture and chronic pain: A criteria-based meta-analysis. Clinical Epidemiology 43:1191–1199, 1990.
5. Ter Riet G, Kleijnen J, Knipschild P. A meta-analysis of studies into the effect of acupuncture on addiction. British Journal of General Practice 40:379–382, 1990.
6. Beyerstein BL, Sampson W. Traditional Medicine and Pseudoscience in China: A Report of the Second CSICOP Delegation (Part 1). Skeptical Inquirer 20(4):18–26, 1996.
7. American Medical Association Council on Scientific Affairs. Reports of the Council on Scientific Affairs of the American Medical Association, 1981. Chicago, 1982, The Association.

8. Ulett GA. Acupuncture update 1984. Southern Medical Journal 78:233234, 1985.

9. Tang J-L, Zhan S-Y, Ernst E. Review of randomised controlled trials of traditional Chinese medicine. British Medical Journal 319:160–161, 1999.

10. Streitberger K, Kleinhenz J. Introducing a placebo needle into acupuncture research. Lancet 352:364–365, 1998.

11. Streitberger K and others. Acupuncture compared to placebo-acupuncture for postoperative nausea and vomiting prophylaxis: A randomised placebo-controlled patient and observer blind trial. Anesthesia 59:142–149, 2004.

12. Norheim JA, Fennebe V. Adverse effects of acupuncture. Lancet 345:1576, 1995.

13. Yamashita H and others. Adverse events related to acupuncture. JAMA 280:1563–1564, 1998.

14. White A and others. Adverse events following acupuncture: Prospective surgery of 32,000 consultations with doctors and physiotherapists. BMJ 323:485–486, 2001.

15. MacPherson H and others. York acupuncture safety study: Prospective survey of 24,000 treatments by traditional acupuncturists. BMJ 323:486–487, 2001.

16. Vincent C. The safety of acupuncture. BMJ 323:467–468, 2001.

17. Acupuncture needle status changed. FDA Talk Paper T96-21, April 1, 1996

18. Wells D. Think acu-practic: Acupuncture benefits for chiropractic. Journal of the American Chiropractic Association 35(3):10–13, 1998.

19. NCCAOM 25th Anniversary Booklet. Burtonsville, MD: NCCAOM, 2007.

20. Department of Education, Office of Postsecondary Education. Nationally Recognized Accrediting Agencies and Associations. Criteria and Procedures for

Listing by the U.S. Secretary For Education and Current List. Washington, D.C., 1995, U.S. Department of Education.

21. Sampson W and others. Acupuncture: The position paper of the National Council Against Health Fraud. Clinical Journal of Pain 7:162–166, 1991.

22. Acupuncture. NIH Consensus Statement 15:(5), November 3–5, 1997.

23. Sampson W. On the National Institute of Drug Abuse Consensus Conference on Acupuncture. Scientific Review of Alternative Medicine 2(1):54–55, 1998.

24. Kalauokalani D and others. Acupuncture for chronic low back pain: Diagnosis and treatment patterns among acupuncturists evaluating the same patient. Southern Medical Journal 94:486–492, 2001.

25. Hogeboom CJ and others. Variation in diagnosis and treatment of chronic low back pain by traditional Chinese medicine acupuncturists. Complementary Therapies in Medicine 9:154–166, 2001.

26. Sherman KJ and others. The diagnosis and treatment of patients with chronic low-back pain by traditional Chinese medical acupuncturists. Alternative and Complementary Medicine 7:641–650, 2001.

27. Zhang GG and others. The variability of TCM pattern diagnosis and herbal prescription on rheumatoid arthritis patients. Alternative Therapies in Health and Medicine 10:58–63, 2004.

28. Zhang GG and others. Variability in the traditional Chinese medicine (TCM) diagnoses and herbal prescriptions provided by three TCM practitioners for 40 patients with rheumatoid arthritis. Alternative Therapies in Health and Medicine 11:415–421, 2005.

29. Coetaux RR and others. Variability in the diagnosis and point selection for persons with frequent headache by traditional Chinese medicine acupuncturists. Alternative and Complementary Medicine 12:863–872, 2006.

Natural Remedies Are Effective Against Migraines

Hillari Dowdle

The author of this viewpoint, Hillari Dowdle, is a writer and editor whose articles have appeared in *Yoga Journal*, *Natural Health*, *Vegetarian Times*, and *Natural Solutions*. According to Dowdle, the unpredictability of migraines requires that they be treated from several angles. Dietary approaches include detoxification of the digestive and lymphatic systems and the ingestion of natural supplements that prevent or reduce migraine symptoms. Different kinds of bodywork, including acupuncture, craniosacral therapy, massage, and biofeedback, improve blood flow and correct misalignments that contribute to headaches, Dowdle notes. Relaxation tools, such as footbaths and still point inducers, can also help to make migraine pain more bearable once an attack has started.

I'm one of nearly 30 million Americans who suffer from the painful, disorienting, and life-disrupting headaches known as migraines. No matter what else is going on in my day, I'm subject to being hijacked at

SOURCE: Hillari Dowdle, "6 Ways to Manage Migraines," *Natural Health*, 39.4, April 2009, pp. 52–56. Reprinted by permission.

any moment by one of these blinding, full-body attacks. A storm moves in? So does a migraine. Music too loud? Throbbing agony. A glass of red wine? A whiff of cologne? A stressful week? You guessed it: headache, headache, headache.

The Migraine Brain

Migraine pain. "Think of your migraine as a wave," says Carolyn Bernstein, M.D., assistant professor of neurology at Harvard Medical School and author of *The Migraine Brain* (2008). "When one hits, it sets off a cascade of cellular events throughout the brain, triggering responses that may differ from a regular headache. For some people, it's nausea; for others, it's pain in the face and jaw."

Migraine traits. No two migraines are alike: You may experience auras, or vomiting, or widespread muscle pain, or dizziness, or sinus pressure, or ringing in the ears, or even partial paralysis. Or not. But there is one underlying constant: hyper-excitability. "In the brain of a migraine sufferer, the neurons are unstable and more susceptible to being triggered," explains Bernstein.

Migraine causes. The list of migraine triggers includes—but is not limited to—barometric pressure changes, too much or too little sleep, stress, bright sunlight, intense heat or cold, muscular tension, hormonal shifts, loud noises, chemical odors or perfumes, overexertion, and a broad range of foods that includes aged cheese, chocolate, caffeine, canned foods, artificial sweeteners, MSG [monosodium glutamate], red wine, beer, and processed foods of all sorts.

Gaining Control

Migraine management. A lucky few will be able to identify one or two triggers. For most of us, it's not so clear. "It could be a bit of misalignment, a bit of toxicity, or a little digestive problem," says James Sensenig, N.D., founding

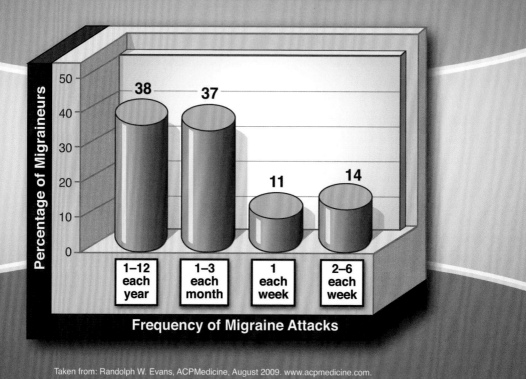

Frequency of Migraine Attacks

Percentage of Migraineurs

Value	Frequency
38	1–12 each year
37	1–3 each month
11	1 each week
14	2–6 each week

Frequency of Migraine Attacks

Taken from: Randolph W. Evans, ACPMedicine, August 2009. www.acpmedicine.com.

president of the American Association of Naturopathic Physicians. Because of their variability, migraines are best treated from several angles including body alignment, diet, and emotions. Here are six of the best strategies:

1. *Track triggers.* "People often don't realize how many headaches they're having," says Audrey Halpern, M.D., holistic neurologist and founder of Manhattan Headache and Neurology. "It's only when you understand how often you get them and what might be causing them that you can start to work toward natural balance." And keeping a diary or journal is a great way to understand your particular triggers and headache patterns, says Halpern.

Chart everything. Note all the conditions leading up to the headache—including weather patterns, menstrual cycle, and stress load—and see what patterns emerge. You can download a migraine diary form at Halpern's website, audreyhalpern.com.

2. *Detox your digestive system.* Ayurveda, India's traditional system of medicine, believes ingestion is a key factor in chronic headaches, so practitioners emphasize detoxification. "A migraine is a sign that the digestive system isn't removing waste effectively," says John Douillard, D.C., Ph.D., director of the LifeSpa Ayurveda center in Boulder, Colo. He likens the problem to a clogged drain. "If you have too much mucus in your intestinal tract, the drains can get clogged, which creates toxicity in the lymph, resulting in dilated blood vessels—or headache."

Sip a tea tonic. To lubricate the intestinal lining, drink tea with demulcent [soothing] herbs—like slippery elm, marshmallow, or licorice—every day, says Douillard. To clean your lymphatic system, take sips of hot water every 15 minutes for two weeks.

3. *Use acupuncture.* Acupuncture—using needles to stimulate certain energy points on the body—can have the same effect as Imitrex and other triptan anti-migraine drugs. Both release chemicals that cause blood vessels to constrict, says William Reddy, L.Ac., Dipl.Ac., spokesperson for the American Association of Acupuncture and Oriental Medicine.

Needles last longer. Unlike medications, which wear off, "acupuncture teaches the blood vessels to stay toned so that over time you don't have migraines anymore," Reddy adds. Most people find relief in four to eight sessions, he says, noting that acupuncture has been effective for 85 to 90 percent of his patients. A meta-analysis published in the journal *Anesthesia and Analgesia* found that acupuncture worked to relieve migraines more often than not.

4. *Get realigned.* "Migraines are often caused by structural issues in the soft tissues surrounding the dural tube, which houses the fluid that nourishes the brain

and spinal cord," says Sheryl McGavin, of the Upledger Institute in Florida. "With craniosacral therapy, you can remove restrictions so the system flows freely." During a session, a practitioner uses a light touch to make adjustments on the head, neck, and upper thorax. Find a certified therapist near you through Upledger's International Association of Healthcare Practitioners (iahp.com).

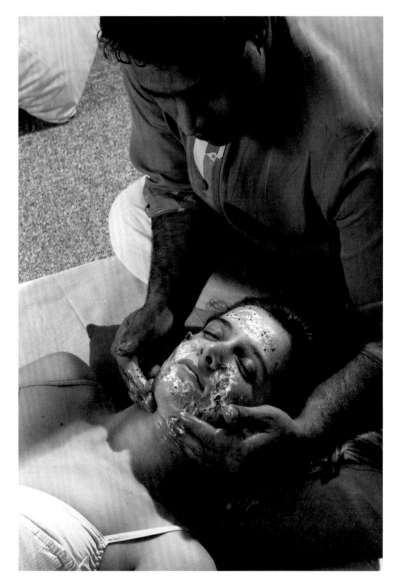

An ayurveda practitioner massages a woman's face using an herbal cream. This ancient Indian medical philosophy seeks to prevent diseases through diet, massage, and exercise. (Mauro Fermariello/Photo Researchers, Inc.)

Other options: Bodywork and massage also help you relax, improve blood flow, and correct misalignments that contribute to headaches.

5. *Try biofeedback therapy.* No matter what triggers your migraines, or how they manifest, stress makes everything worse, says James Gordon, M.D., founder of the Center for Mind-Body Medicine in Washington, D.C. He suggests a type of biofeedback therapy that measures body temperature: When you're stressed and more likely to have migraines your hands grow cold. With these biofeedback devices, you can learn to warm your hands and raise your body temperature, which reduces stress.

Go with a pro. To find a certified biofeedback practitioner, go to healthfinder.gov.

Herbs, Vitamins, and Minerals

6. *Take supplements.* One of the best long-term prevention strategies is to take natural supplements. Try these one at a time for at least three months to determine whether they're working for you:

> **Gut Brain Therapy**: You can trigger-proof your digestive tract with Gut Brain Therapy's two-part protocol, which works to strengthen the enteric nervous system housed in your gut. The Foundation Formula "feeds" the gut with easily digestible proteins derived from fish, and the Renew Formula stimulates liver and kidney function with an herbal blend that includes milk thistle, dandelion, beet root, and artichoke.
> *Research*: A small study published in *Alternative Medicine Review* found that 80 percent of the participants who took Gut Brain supplements for three months reported improvements in migraine frequency and severity.
> *Dosage*: Follow label guidelines.
>
> **Coenzyme Q10**: It's not clear exactly how the vitamin-like substance known as CoQ10 works—it might

improve the brain's ability to metabolize glucose, Halpern hypothesizes.

Research: A study published in the journal *Neurology* found that CoQ10 could reduce migraine frequency by up to 50 percent.

Dosage: 100 mg, three times a day.

Magnesium: This simple mineral has muscle-relaxing properties and may stave off a migraine by preventing blood vessel spasms, notes Maureen Williams, N.D., a naturopath in private practice on Cortes Island, British Columbia.

Research: In a study published in the journal *Cephalalgia*, patients who took magnesium every day for 12 weeks reported significantly fewer migraine attacks (versus those taking a placebo) after only nine weeks.

Dosage: 600 mg a day, says the *Cephalalgia* study.

Butterbur: The herb butterbur stabilizes the cells that produce histamine, so it's a good choice for those who also suffer from allergies, says Debra Brammer, N.D., clinical dean of naturopathic medicine at Bastyr University. Look for products such as Petadolex that are free of pyrrolizidine alkaloids (potentially toxic compounds).

Research: The herb was shown to significantly reduce migraine frequency in some people, according to a study in the journal *Neurology*.

Dosage: 100 mg, three to four times a day.

Feverfew: "This herb may work by inhibiting the inflammation cascade and stabilizing substance P, the neurotransmitter responsible for the pain response," Brammer says.

Research: Clinical studies are mixed but feverfew has been used as a migraine treatment in folk medicine.

Dosage: 100 mg, three times a day.

Methods and Tools That Soothe

Warm your feet. Soak your feet in a hot water footbath or tub to draw blood away from your head and reduce a migraine. . . .

Try these creature comforts to offset problematic symptoms, and make migraine pain more bearable:

> *Still point inducer.* When you feel a headache coming on, lie down for 15 minutes with the back of your head on a still point inducer, a small device with two mounds that cradle your skull. The device mimics the effects of craniosacral therapy: Your weight provides gentle pressure to improve blood flow, correct misalignment, and help you relax. . . .

> *Foot bath.* Warming the feet can help draw blood flow away from the head and relieve pain, says Ronald Stram, M.D., founder of the Center for Integrative Health and Healing. While you toast your tootsies, chill a pair of thin cotton socks in ice water. When you're done soaking (at least ten minutes), wring out the socks and put them on your feet. Then cover with a pair of warm, woolen socks. The body will now start warming your feet, and in two or three hours, your head will hurt less. . . .

> # FAST FACT
>
> According to the Gale Health and Wellness Resource Center, celery juice, ginger, oil of rosemary, and riboflavin supplements may help prevent migraine attacks.

Migraine Medications

If natural solutions aren't working, consider one of these prescribed medications:

> *Preventives.* Anti-seizure drugs like Topamax or Depakote, low-dose antidepressants, anti-nausea drugs, anti-inflammatories, or heart medications can keep migraines at bay, but finding the right drug is hit-or-miss and side effects can include weight gain, foggy brain, and hair loss.

Abortives. A class of drugs called triptans (such as Imitrex or Zomig) can halt a migraine in its tracks, but can cost $25 or more per dose.

Rescuers. Opiates (such as Percocet or Vicodin) or short-acting barbiturates (such as Fioricet) can bring short-term relief by masking pain but may be habit-forming and can cause lightheadedness and other side effects.

Plastic Surgery Can Ease Migraines

Catherine Saint Louis

Plastic surgery can significantly reduce the number of headaches that some migraine sufferers experience, reports Catherine Saint Louis in the following article. In recent years, surgeon Bahman Guyuron began hearing reports about improvement of migraine symptoms from some of his patients who had undergone forehead lifts. With further exploration, Saint Louis says, he discovered that surgery on trigger points in either the temples, forehead, or the back of the head reduced the frequency of headaches among most of his migraine patients. Some experts caution, however, that the surgery is effective only for those who can identify triggering points of irritation—which is a minority of migraineurs. But those who experience chronic, uncontrollable migraines may make good candidates for this surgery, the author points out. Saint Louis is an editor at the *New York Times*.

Many of the nearly 30 million Americans who suffer from migraines end up feeling like guinea pigs. Chronic patients—those who are laid low 15 or more days a month—often cycle through drug

SOURCE: Catherine Saint Louis, "Plastic Surgery May Also Ease Migraines," *New York Times*, September 3, 2009, p. E3 (L). Reprinted by permission.

after drug in search of relief. They also contend with side effects like mental sluggishness and stomach upset. Treatment involves guesswork because doctors have not pinpointed what causes migraines, nor do they know which drugs will best help which patients.

"It can be a merry-go-round going from medication to medication in pursuit of control," said Dr. Roger K. Cady, the vice president of the board for the National Headache Foundation, a nonprofit organization devoted to patient education.

No wonder that earlier this month [September 2009], news of a surgical "cure" that touts a high success rate ricocheted worldwide. The double-blind study, published in the journal *Plastic and Reconstructive Surgery*, found that more than 80 percent of patients who underwent surgery in one of three "trigger sites" significantly reduced their number of headaches compared with more than 55 percent of the group who had sham surgery. More than half of the patients with the real surgery reported a "complete elimination" of headaches compared with about 4 percent of the placebo group.

A Cosmetic Procedure as a Migraine Cure?

Forehead lifts are cosmetic procedures that plastic surgeons typically perform to smooth furrowed brows. But a decade ago, after some of his patients reported that their migraines improved post-operation, Dr. Bahman Guyuron, a plastic surgeon and the lead author of the study, began to search for a surgical solution that could address migraine trigger points—which he defines as where the headache begins and settles—in the forehead, temples and the back of the head.

Headache specialists tend to be neurologists or internists, so Dr. Guyuron's work has not always been taken seriously. "If I had a neurologist tell me there's a new way of doing a facelift, I would have been very skeptical about it also," said Dr. Guyuron, the chairman of the plastic surgery department at University Hospitals Case Medical Center in Cleveland. "But honestly I would have had an open mind."

In the last month, the press has made much of the fact that a single operation could relieve migraines and turn back the clock in one fell swoop. But it is the potential that surgery for migraines may offer a viable alternative to drugs that has migraine specialists intrigued. "A very large subset became headache-free and remained headache-free for a year—that is a fantastic result," said Dr. Richard B. Lipton, the director of the Montefiore Headache Center in the Bronx.

Especially considering that in the field of migraines, success is defined "as a reduction of 50 percent of attacks," Dr. Cady said. Going from 10 episodes monthly to 5 is a welcome change, he added, but "it's still a lot of migraines."

The Theory Behind the Surgery

The theory behind the surgery is that because some migraines are caused when sensitive nerve branches are squeezed and irritated by muscles, deactivating those muscles could bring prolonged relief. In the off-label use of Botox for migraines, those same muscles—when paralyzed with Botox injections—have eased headaches in some patients for roughly three months. Forehead lifts, Dr. Guyuron reasoned, might result in a longer-lasting, perhaps permanent, alleviation of pain. Only study participants who responded positively to Botox were offered the surgery.

(Dr. Cady cautioned that the research on Botox as a treatment for chronic headaches is not yet ironclad. Allergan, Botox's maker, is pursuing the approval of Botox as a treatment for chronic migraines by the Food and Drug Administration.)

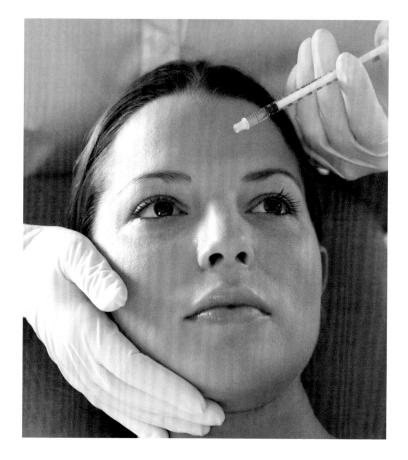

Botox injections in the forehead, which paralyze, irritate, and squeeze muscles, have been found to ease migraine pain for up to three months in some patients. (**Adam Gault**/ **Photo Researchers**, Inc.)

Many headache specialists, Dr. Lipton and Dr. Cady included, emphasize that this migraine surgery isn't applicable to most sufferers. "Folks who are appropriate for this procedure—they are the tip of the iceberg, not the vast majority," said Dr. Jennifer S. Kriegler, a neurologist who is one of the study's authors and who works at the Cleveland Clinic's headache center.

At this stage, suitable candidates are those who endure frequent migraines and have failed more tried-and-true methods of controlling their headaches, several doctors said. The bottom line, Dr. Lipton explained, is if you can't identify a point of irritation and "if you don't respond to Botox, we don't know if this treatment works for you."

Doctors' Concerns

Some doctors fear that the surgery may be offered to inappropriate patients before further research confirms its efficacy for a broader group of patients. "I don't want us to overshoot and start doing widespread surgeries in not very well selected patients until we are convinced this is broadly effective," said Dr. F. Michael Cutrer, the chief of the headache division in the neurology department at the Mayo Clinic in Rochester, Minn. "You can always stop a medication but you can't reverse a surgery."

As word of the surgery spreads, Dr. Cutrer said that he anticipated pleas for referrals to the few plastic surgeons nationwide who offer the operations, but that "until we maybe have studies that are a bit larger, and some longer follow-up I'm going to be very cautious."

So far, Dr. Guyuron has trained roughly 150 doctors, and other plastic surgeons are refining their own migraine operations, even though they barely advertise.

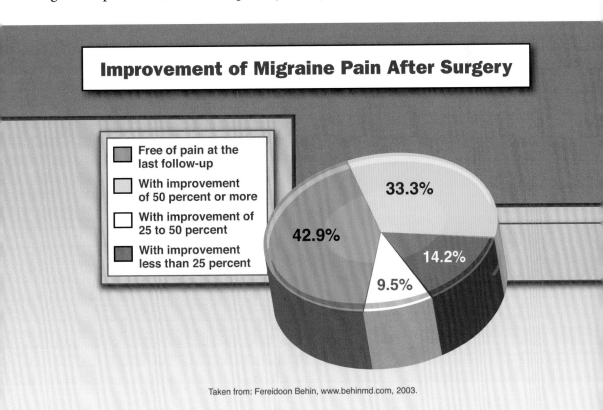

Improvement of Migraine Pain After Surgery

- Free of pain at the last follow-up
- With improvement of 50 percent or more
- With improvement of 25 to 50 percent
- With improvement less than 25 percent

33.3%

42.9%

14.2%

9.5%

Taken from: Fereidoon Behin, www.behinmd.com, 2003.

A Godsend for Some

Two years ago [in 2007], an aunt told Shannon Byrne, from Mayfield Heights, Ohio, about Dr. Guyuron's migraine surgery. Ms. Byrne said that she had already spent a decade on "every single medication you can think of." Still, pain hammered her head more days than not. "You're willing to try anything," she said. Dr. Guyuron's surgery, which she had 18 months ago, was a godsend. The migraines that led to her dropping out of college and to a stroke at 20 are gone. "My dad told me not to worry about the money," Ms. Byrne, now 22, said of the thousands paid out of pocket.

A classic forehead lift for cosmetic effect differs significantly from surgery for migraine sufferers. The latter removes frown muscles more thoroughly and entails padding nerves with fatty tissue, said Dr. David A. Branch, a plastic surgeon in Bangor, Me., who performs migraine operations.

Sometimes, migraine surgery doesn't involve the forehead at all. It varies according to where the patient's trigger sites are: forehead, temples or back of the head. If Dr. Guyuron operates on the temples, the eyebrows are rejuvenated, he said. It is only the surgery at the back of the head that has no added perk, he said.

It's unclear whether or not the migraine sufferers whose pain had disappeared a year post-operation will remain headache-free for life.

"My goal is zero headaches," said Dr. Jeffrey E. Janis, a plastic surgeon in Dallas, who has performed roughly 100 operations in the last five years after training with Dr. Guyuron. "I might be able to achieve that in some, not in all."

Complete elimination is "a pretty strong claim after one year of follow-up," Dr. Cutrer said.

As a way of dampening expectations, Dr. Kriegler, who has referred patients to Dr. Guyuron, frequently tells them: "Once a migraineur, always a migraineur."

CHAPTER 3

Living with Migraines

Facing a Fear of Needles to Ease Migraine Pain

Gretchen Roberts

In the following selection writer Gretchen Roberts tells the story of her ongoing struggles with migraines, which were first triggered when she began taking oral contraceptives. Even after she stopped taking the birth control pills, her migraines continued. The drug that her doctor prescribed for her left her with nausea and muscle weakness, so she decided to stop taking that as well. Even though Roberts was afraid of needles, her desperation led her to seek out help from an acupuncturist. After a series of appointments, her migraine attacks became less intense and occurred less frequently.

A t 22, I started getting migraines. Simultaneously, I had just started taking birth control pills, which a well-meaning family doctor had prescribed to try and ease my menstrual cramps. While I didn't notice a discernable difference in my cramps' severity, an ominous change was taking place in my body.

SOURCE: Gretchen Roberts, "Gaining Control: After Years of Migraine Suffering, One Woman Faces Her Needle Fears and Challenges Her Spiky Headaches," *Better Nutrition*, March 1, 2006, pp. 46–50. Reprinted by permisison.

Photo on previous page. Migraine sufferers can experience frustration when attempting to get their headaches properly diagnosed and treated. (Phanie/ Photo Researchers, Inc.)

Though my mother suffered from migraines, I was a typically unobservant child, oblivious to her malady. So when my headaches began, I called them "spiky headaches" for lack of a medical term. Besides the feeling that someone had driven a gigantic nail into the side of my head, I felt nauseated and weak. My back, neck, jaw and arm muscles on the offending side would tense up like tightly wound coils, as if they'd been pulled too hard during a grueling workout.

For more than three years I suffered through numerous spiky headaches that gradually increased in length, frequency and intensity. Finally, I'd had enough. I began to research the headaches. Not only did I realize what I had and that I'd inherited them from my mother, I was sure the cause of my migraines was the hormones in the birth control. My first step was to get off the pill.

Medication Brings Some Relief, with Side Effects

But the migraines continue fast and fierce, and I developed little ways of coping with the throes of pain: icing my eyes, rubbing my jaw, strictly regulating my sleep, eating regular meals and sipping white wine for a tiny bit of immediate relief.

Well into my fourth year of migraine suffering, I finally went to see my doctor. She confirmed the birth control was probably the trigger, but given my family's history— I'd learned that not only my mom but my aunt too had migraines—I likely didn't have a chance. She handed me a prescription for Maxalt, a drug that constricts the swollen blood vessels around the brain that cause the painful throbbing associated with migraines.

The catch with Maxalt, is that, like other migraine medications, you must take it almost before the migraine starts for it to be effective. I had difficulty taking the pill early enough, preferring to pretend a migraine wasn't on

> **FAST FACT**
>
> Patient Health International reports that migraine is three times more common in women than in men.

the horizon. When I did take it on time, the drug took away the migraine pain but left a sickening nausea and muscle weakness in its wake. I always felt much sicker after taking the medication. Whether the nausea was from the migraine, the Maxalt, or both, I wasn't sure. But the weakness was definitely from the drug; in fact, it's a listed side effect. In addition to working on the migraine, it affects the whole body. All these side effects were merely the sunny side of hell.

Trying Something New

The day I listened to my mother and aunt chat about how often they popped migraine pills (up to five a week), I knew I had to get off the drug for the sake of my long-term health.

So a year ago I booked my first appointment with an acupuncturist, despite being deathly afraid of needles. (To give you some idea of my fear: I insisted on an all-natural birth with my daughter because I preferred birthing pain to a needle prick in my back.) I'd done my homework, though, and read studies showing acupuncture can reduce, if not eliminate, migraine frequency and intensity. Besides the risk of being maimed by tiny needles, what did I have to lose?

The first session was a two-hour affair. My acupuncturist spent an hour asking questions about my migraines: What seems to trigger them, how often I get them, how long they last, where they start, how they progress and possible environmental causes. We also discussed my life: the joys and the stresses, as both can set off head pain.

I also mentioned my needle phobia several times. As I lay face down on the table and she began inserting needles into my back and shoulders, she asked probing questions about my work, my daughter—anything to keep me distracted. I was mildly surprised when she dimmed the lights and said she'd be back in 20 minutes. She kept me so busy talking that I wasn't focused on the needles and suddenly she was done. It wasn't as bad as I'd imagined.

Next I lay on my back, and the acupuncturist inserted needles into my knees, wrists and feet. In one word: ouch. There's not a lot of fat to cushion the prick in those sensitive spots. But it was over in 20 more minutes, and I was free for two weeks. That evening's prescription was no alcohol, no sex and no exercise—fine with me, since I was curiously wiped out from the whole thing. Apparently, it's common to feel deeply relaxed or even somewhat disoriented after the initial one or two treatments.

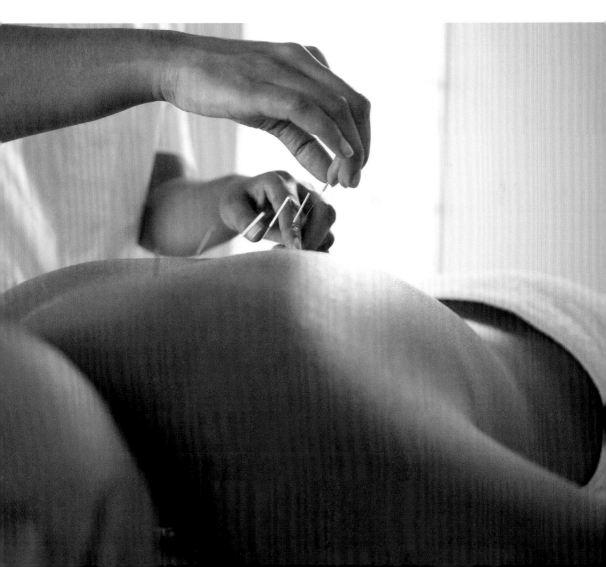

Overcoming her acute fear of needles, the author elected to begin acupuncture treatments. Relief was gradual, but the intensity of her migraines was reduced. (**Adam Gault/ Photo Researchers, Inc.**)

The first treatment wasn't a cure-all. Nothing specific happened—it was a gradual thing.

Less Frequent Migraines

My series of appointments gradually lengthened from two weeks between each visit to three, then four, then six, and I charted my migraines along the way. They basically tapered from frequent and fierce to fewer and less painful. Some months I had just one, significantly down from the six or seven before acupuncture. Other months didn't go as well, but I was always able to pinpoint specific triggers, such as a major change in atmospheric pressure or a period-related hormonal swing.

The migraines I get now are less intense. Instead of being confined to bed for 24 hours to sleep off a nasty one, I sometimes find a migraine will wear itself out by evening. Often I can semifunction, taking care of my daughter and putting dinner on the table in slow, measured steps. As debilitating as that sounds, any migraine sufferer will vouch that just being capable of getting out of bed is a major improvement.

I still hold out hope that a safe, permanent cure for migraines will be found in my lifetime, but until that happens, I'll stick with what works for me even if it involves dozens of sharp little needles.

A Lifelong Journey with Migraines

"Nancy"

The author of the following viewpoint, "Nancy," shares her story at the Migraine Research Foundation website as part of its campaign to raise awareness and to fund scientific research. Nancy's migraines began when she was in high school and increased in frequency when she married and began taking birth control pills. At the time there were no medications for migraines, and the only thing that gave her relief from the pain was sleep. Over time she learned what foods triggered her attacks, and she discovered some mildly helpful home remedies. These remedies would be of no help once her vomiting started, however. Nancy's coworkers did not understand the severity of her attacks, and she had trouble retaining employment because of her migraines. Currently Nancy continues to experience migraines, although they are less severe now that she is postmenopausal.

I began having headaches in high school. I remember vividly those that began in the spring, just as the weather began to change, and school was almost over for the year. I endured the afternoon, longing for

SOURCE: "Nancy," "For Sufferers: Migraine Stories," Migraine Research Foundation. Reprinted by permission.

the time when I would get home and could place my head on the pillow. My sister played the piano which was against a shared wall with my bedroom. My pleas for the noise to stop were not taken seriously, and my parents failed to intervene. Even though I missed dinner with the family and stayed in my room trying to sleep it off, no one realized the agony I was suffering. No one took me to the doctor, as no one went to the doctor for a headache! My pessimistic grandmother murmured that I was going to die young. To her credit, she was the only one who seemed to know the gravity of my suffering.

I married at 19 and began taking birth control pills. The headaches increased to at least three times a week. The headaches would start at work in the afternoon, and by the time I arrived at home, sometimes driving in the heat with no air conditioning in bumper-to-bumper traffic, I had a full-blown headache with vomiting. I did not have any medication to take. The only thing that helped was to go to sleep. Somehow, while asleep, the pain left, and my brain could rest.

Finally, an OB/GYN [obstetrician and gynecologist] told me that birth control pills worsen migraines. He referred me to a neurologist. Fearing a brain tumor or worse, I was concerned about numbness on one side of my face which preceded a headache. He told me that I was having a migraine. He tried to encourage me by telling me that highly intelligent people have migraines, and that we are perfectionists. There were no medications at that time (1967) for migraine relief.

Multiple Triggers

Cigarette smoke sent me straight to bed with the worst of the headaches. At that time, everyone seemed to smoke. I was required to go to after-hour office functions. There was lots of drinking and smoking, neither of which I did. It seemed those who partook of the drinks and cigarettes

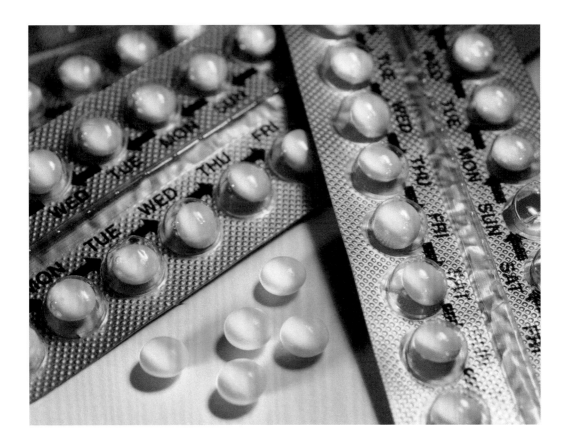

Like many women who take birth control pills, the author's migraine headaches increased in frequency when she began taking the contraceptive. (**Cordelia Molloy/Photo Researchers, Inc.**)

were fine, but I would miss the next day of work with a super migraine.

I had never seen a list of foods to avoid, but over time, I found that onions, cheese, peanut butter, and dough-nuts gave me a headache. I had my own little remedies: Vick's Salve, Cheetos, Ginger Ale and an ice bag. Later, I found that other sufferers had their own lists of discov-ered remedies: tea with lemon, heating pad, nasal spray, etc. But when the vomiting started, nothing helped. I have stopped on the side of the road and vomited in the gutter, had to stop at a friend's house because I could drive no further, thrown up in the trash can at my desk, and thrown up in a bag in my car on the way to church. I have visited with family holding an ice bag on my head and worn sunglasses at my desk.

Skeptical Coworkers

My children have had to stay in the house and take care of me. While in elementary school, each of my children already knew what to do for Mama: prepare an ice bag, keep the blinds drawn, answer the phone, watch TV quietly in another room, tell friends they cannot come over, and make their own lunch.

So, for years, I lost days of my life, missed family get-togethers, parts of vacations, and days from work. Co-workers did not understand. Many would make a point, and still do, of telling me they have a headache, so as to say "see, I am at work, suffering with my headache." For a Christmas present, I once received a "pill box" for my headache medication. This was supposed to be funny. I lost one job after 5 months because I was out with a headache, vomiting, etc. The boss called my house to check up on me. My son answered the phone, not knowing who was calling, but told him that I was sleeping. I had finally stopped vomiting, and my son was not about to wake me up. The next day, my boss accused me, and thus my son, of lying. He said he called my house, and my son told him I was sleeping, but that I really must not have been home. So he fired me.

My current job of 20 years is very demanding, but my boss has migraines and has been sympathetic for the most part. One of his friends is now my neurologist, who specializes in migraines and suffers [from them] himself. He has helped me more than anyone.

> **FAST FACT**
>
> According to WebMD, between 60 and 70 percent of female migraine sufferers report that their migraines are related to their menstrual cycles.

Still Suffering

I am 61 years old and still have migraines. Completing menopause has helped me, as well as learning what not to do, or what to do, and how to take medications properly.

I still have memories of migraines, and how much of my life I missed while suffering.

Now, my granddaughter, age 8, has frequent headaches. I have given her parents all of the information I have concerning children's headaches. God forbid that she has migraines, but if she does, I want her to get proper treatment and avoid the misery that her Mimi has suffered.

The best part of a migraine is when it leaves you. The next day I might feel a little washed out, but I survived.

A Migraine Sufferer's Barometer Is in Her Head

Richard Brookhiser

Richard Brookhiser is a journalist, biographer, historian, and senior editor at the biweekly magazine *National Review*. In the following essay he sympathetically explores his wife's battle with migraines, describing some of the specialists and treatments she has tried. Botox injections provide relief for a time; she also gets anesthetic injected into trigger points in her head and takes training in the Alexander technique, a posture program that improves health. The approach of rain sets off her migraines, as does the noisy bustle of city life, writes Brookhiser.

The English cartoonist James Gillray drew a famous panel titled "The Gout." The wordless image showed a naked human foot, bitten by a tiny demon. How would he illustrate "Headache"? Years ago, my wife and I saw a modern dance piece called "The Garden of Earthly Delights," based on paintings by Hieronymus Bosch. At one point a man engaged in a pointless,

SOURCE: Richard Brookhiser, "Skull Session," *National Review,* July 20, 2009, p. 51. Reprinted by permission.

maniacal struggle with another[,] jammed his opponent's head up against one side of a bass drum, and pounded the other side. That might do.

My wife suffers from migraines. I don't, but I have seen enough of hers to bless all sufferers. The head itself seems to be infected from the inside. You don't want to sleep, because when you wake there is no change. You are compelled to toss and turn, but tossing and turning give no relief. Pain is compounded by hopelessness. Since no one ever has just one migraine, each new one holds out the prospect of endless repetition. A migraine thrusts life into an old world and a police state, where the gates of heaven are shut against you.

Migraineurs in New York City

This being the city [New York City], there are head-ache specialists to consult (until HMOs [health mainte-nance organizations] and Obamacare [President Barack Obama's health care plans] drive them out of business). My wife's is a tall, serious man, originally a Soviet Jew, with an office on the Upper East Side. His waiting room is the Lourdes [a site in France known for pilgrimages and alleged miraculous healing] of migraine sufferers. Never have I seen a collection of patients so silent, so downcast. Most of them are women, proving yet again that men relieve their tensions with alcohol, violence, and meaningless sex. The wall art aims to soothe—one painting shows a grape arbor, with a red apple hanging miraculously among its fellow fruits. It is the fruit of the Tree of Relief—eat it, and you will have knowledge of Good and No More Evil. No one in the waiting room can stir herself to look at it.

This doctor's technique is to inject the forehead, tem-ples, and shoulders with Botox. Botox is best known as the weapon of vanity against time. If you don't go in for nips and tucks and Chinese eyes, Botox is the other way to hold facial wrinkles at bay. After 40 we are all supposed to have the faces we deserve. And so it is of those who get themselves injected with Botox—their faces are bland, puffed, and wiped like a crashed hard drive of all the information of experience. And yet Botox can also fight migraines by paralyzing muscles that go into spasm. My wife's doctor's way with a needle is disconcertingly freehand—he pricks there, there, and there, like a conductor cuing pizzicato [a plucking technique on string instruments]. Normally these cures last for three months; my wife's headaches, tough customers, start creeping back after ten weeks.

No self-respecting city-dweller has only one specialist on call—that would be like knowing only one restaurant—and another doctor my wife turns to from time to time uses another technique: injecting mild anesthetic into knots of muscles called trigger points. This causes them to relax, and my wife to relax. This doctor is a merry badger, happy to discuss Bernie Madoff [a stock broker convicted of fraud] or other figures of the moment as he plies his healing arts. His office is near the U.N. [United Nations headquarters], and [his] waiting room, like his colleague's, is a Pool of Bethesda [a holy healing site in Jerusalem], crowded with glum sufferers, despairing of either Jesus or the angel.

The Alexander Technique

A third way of fighting headaches is the universal solution to all problems: Change your life. In the case of migraines, it involves changing how you walk, stand, and carry yourself. The Alexander technique is a posture program developed by an actor at the turn of the last century who found his voice going; he decided to tinker with his instrument, got his voice back, and spawned a movement. Actors and singers remain disciples to this day; my wife has found an instructor on Union Square. This is a remedy for the long haul, like fighting the jihad [Islamic extremists] by promoting democracy, though it may work best in the end.

An aching head makes a new map of the city, with highlights at all the addresses where relief is to be found.

It joins the sheaf of maps that show the ways to fresh vegetables, leg presses, socks, work, art, drinks, 24-hour pharmacies, and ATMs. If you copied them all together into one map it would be as dense as the Talmud [a central text of Judaism].

Predicting Weather

Different circumstances appear to set migraines off, or to exacerbate them. One is the approach of rain. My wife's barometer is her head. She can predict the weather as well as a field full of cows (standing, clear; sitting, rain); better than human meteorologists. When we see, out our apartment window, or down a vista of side street, a black cloud dragging its heavy udder along, she says, "You see that cloud? It's inside my head." This month, an anthology of unseasonable showers, drizzles, and downpours, has been a particular trial.

One other factor surely is the bustle of city life. The very density that supplies an array of cures creates the need for them. What the city gives with the right hand, it filches with the left. Take the background of jackhammers, ambulances, garbage trucks, barflies, cell-phone yakkers, subways taking the curve into Union Square, and barking news readers on the driver's-seat screens in taxi cabs, and add, in the supposed refuge of your apartment, someone drilling—a molly bolt? an oil well?—in the apartment upstairs, and the clenched muscles and swollen veins of the neck and head exchange glances and say, "Time to party!"

And yet Thomas Jefferson, bard of the soil and president in a capital [Washington, DC] that, if it was better than a pigsty, was still not a real city, had headaches too. "Fits," he called them, and they kept him in a dark room from nine to five for three weeks at a time. If he suffered what I have seen, I say let him have Sally [Hemings, one of his slaves].

> **FAST FACT**
>
> The journal *Headache* reports that as many as 50 percent of migraines are weather related.

GLOSSARY

abdominal migraine   A type of migraine, mostly affecting children and teens, that involves abdominal pain and vomiting but little or no headache.

abortive medication   A medicine that stops the migraine process before debilitating symptoms take hold. It is most effective when taken at the very first sign of an approaching migraine.

acupuncture   A form of traditional Chinese medicine that involves the insertion of very fine needles into specific points on the body. Used to correct imbalances that lead to illness and to decrease or eliminate pain.

analgesic   Pain-relieving medication.

aura   A warning sign that a migraine is about to begin, usually occurring about ten to thirty minutes before the onset of the migraine. Usually includes visual disturbances, such as flashing lights, blurred vision, or zigzag lines, along with numbness, motor weakness, and speech difficulties.

barbiturate   A prescription medicine that causes relaxation and sedation.

biofeedback   A mental stress–reduction process that increases an individual's control over certain physiological states such as tension and pain response.

Botox®   An injectable form of the botulinum toxin used to prevent chronic headaches in adults.

caffeine   A stimulant found in coffee, tea, cola, and chocolate and a common ingredient in over-the-counter medications for tension-type headaches and migraines.

chronic headache   A headache that occurs fifteen days per month over a period of three to six months.

cluster headaches Sudden, severe headaches that occur in a closely grouped pattern several times a day over a period of two weeks to three months. Not considered migraine, this is the rarest form of headache disorder.

common migraine Migraine without aura.

cortical spreading depression A wave of decreased brain activity that slowly moves from the back to the front of the brain's surface. Some believe this may precede the migraine aura.

ergot derivative drugs Drugs that bind to the neurotransmitter serotonin, thereby decreasing the transmission of pain messages along nerve fibers.

headache diary A form used to record a person's headache symptoms and triggers. Assists health care providers in properly treating headaches.

migraineur A person who suffers from migraine disease.

narcotic Strong prescription pain medication.

neurotransmitters Chemicals in the brain that help nerve cells communicate with each other.

nonsteroidal anti-inflammatory drug (NSAID) A medication that decreases pain and inflammation, such as aspirin or ibuprofen.

postdrome The period following the headache.

premonitory symptom A symptom occurring up to twenty-four hours before the onset of migraine.

preventive medication A drug taken on a daily basis to reduce the frequency and severity of migraines.

primary headache A headache that is not the result of another medical condition. Migraine, cluster, and tension-type headaches are all primary headaches.

rebound headache	A headache caused by the overuse of medications for headache pain.
secondary headache	A headache that is the result of another medical condition, such as sinus- and allergy-related disorders, injuries, or tumors.
serotonin	A neurotransmitter involved in communicating the message to the brain to dilate or constrict blood vessels. The constriction and dilation of blood vessels can stimulate nerves that carry pain messages to the brain, leading to migraine.
status migrainosus	A rare, severe form of migraine lasting seventy-two hours or longer. Requires hospitalization.
tension-type headache	The most common type of headache in adults, generally thought to be caused by tightened muscles in the scalp and back of the neck. Characterized by a squeezing, bandlike pain around the forehead area.
trigeminal nerve	The main sensory nerve of the face.
trigger	Something that brings about a disease or condition.
triptans	A family of drugs used to treat migraines and cluster headaches by preventing or stopping nerve tissue inflammation and resulting blood vessel changes that lead to such headaches.
vascular headache	Headaches characterized by throbbing, pulsating pain caused by the activation of nerve fibers in the wall of certain brain blood vessels. Migraine is one type of vascular headache.

CHRONOLOGY

B.C.   **7000**   Trepanation, the practice of drilling a hole in the head to relieve pain, is used as a headache remedy. (The practice continues into the eighteenth century).

4000   The first known written record of a headache occurs in a Mesopotamian poem.

1550   The oldest medical document, the Ebers Papyrus of Thebes, Egypt, advises rubbing a silurus (an electric catfish) on the side of the head as a treatment for migraine.

400   Greek physician Hippocrates is the first to recognize the aura that frequently precedes migraines. He prescribes bloodletting, leeches, and vomiting as cures for headaches.

A.D.   **ca. 50**   Roman medical writer Aulus Cornelius Celsus is the first to indicate that migraine is a lifelong nonfatal disorder.

ca. 60   Greek doctor Aretaeus of Cappadocia describes migraines as *heterocrania* ("another head")—noting symptoms of pain as well as nausea and vomiting in his book *About Sharp and Chronic Diseases*.

ca. 160   Greco-Roman surgeon Galen defines migraine as *hemicrania*, highlighting the sensation of pain on one side of the head, and claims that changes in blood vessels cause the disorder.

ca. 200   Chinese surgeon Hua T'o uses acupuncture to treat migraine.

1684   In his posthumously published book *Practice of Physick*, English doctor Thomas Willis theorizes that headache pain is related to swollen blood vessels in the head.

1872   British physician Arthur Latham maintains that auras are caused by contraction of the cerebral arteries.

1873   British physician Edward Liveing publishes *On Megrim, Sick-Headache, and Some Allied Disorders*, the first major treatise on migraine.

1886   American pharmacist John Pemberton invents Coca-Cola as a cure for headaches.

1897   German chemist Felix Hoffmann first synthesizes a medically useful form of aspirin.

1929   Ergotamine tartrate is first used for treating migraine.

1941   Amyl nitrite is first used to alleviate migraine aura symptoms.

1943   Brazilian scientist Aristides Leao first describes cortical spreading depression, a brain phenomenon that some believe is a precursor to the migraine aura.

1953   The analgesic acetaminophen is marketed in the United States by the Sterling-Winthrop Company.

1962   The US National Institutes of Health develops diagnostic criteria for migraine, recognizing classical migraine (with aura) and common migraine (without aura).

1969 The analgesic ibuprofen is made available in the United Kingdom.

1970s American singer Elvis Presley is treated for classical migraine disorder. He struggled with addictions to the narcotics prescribed for his headaches.

1988 The International Headache Society classifies cluster headache as a distinct headache disorder—no longer defining it as a variant of migraine.

1998 The US Food and Drug Administration (FDA) allows Excedrin to be marketed as the first nonprescription drug for mild to moderate migraine pain, which leads to a 17 percent increase in its sales.

1999 A paper published in the British medical journal *Lancet* suggests that migraine hallucinations may have inspired Lewis Carroll's *Alice in Wonderland* and *Through the Looking Glass.*

2004 The FDA approves topiramate as a migraine preventive for adults.

2007 A study published in the journal *Neurology* finds that migraines may have a beneficial effect on memory and cognitive function.

2010 An international scientific study finds the first genetic link to common migraine.

The FDA approves Botox injections as a treatment for chronic migraine.

ORGANIZATIONS TO CONTACT

The editors have compiled the following list of organizations concerned with the issues debated in this book. The descriptions are derived from materials provided by the organizations. All have publications or information available for interested readers. The list was compiled on the date of publication of the present volume; the information provided here may change. Be aware that many organizations take several weeks or longer to respond to inquiries, so allow as much time as possible.

American Academy of Neurology (AAN)
1080 Montreal Ave.
Saint Paul, MN 55116
phone: (800) 879-1960
fax: (651) 695-2791
website: www.aan.com

Established in 1948, the AAN is an international professional association of more than twenty-one thousand neurologists and neuroscience professionals who care for patients with neurological disorders. The academy publishes the *Neurology Journal* and the biweekly newsletter *Neurology Today*. Its website offers a searchable archive of fact sheets, news articles, and research summaries, including "Treatment of Migraine Headache in Children and Adolescents" and "Pharmacological Management for Prevention of Migraine."

American Headache Society Committee on Headache Education (ACHE)
19 Mantua Rd., Mount Royal, NJ 08061
phone: (856) 423-0043
fax: (856) 423-0082
e-mail: achehg@talley
.com
website: www.achenet
.org

Created in 1990 through the initiative of the American Headache Society, ACHE is a nonprofit patient-health professional partnership dedicated to advancing the treatment and management of patients with headache. ACHE serves as an educational resource for health care providers who seek patient information materials, tools, and resources to help educate and support their patients and their families who are affected by disabling headache. These educational materials also may be useful to health policy makers, employers, opinion leaders, schools, and families of headache sufferers. Its website offers links to a gallery of art by headache sufferers and an extensive archive of educational articles, including "Headache Hygiene: What Is It?" and "The Migraineur's Bill of Rights."

American Migraine Foundation (AMF)
19 Mantua Rd., Mount Royal, NJ 08061
phone: (856) 423-0043
fax: (856) 423-0082
e-mail: amf@talley.com
website: www.american migrainefoundation.org

An outgrowth of the American Headache Society, the AMF is a nonprofit foundation dedicated to the advancement of migraine research. Its mission is to support innovative studies and investigations that will lead to improvement in the lives of those who suffer from migraine and other disabling headaches. Links to news articles and research reports, including "Migraines and Obesity" and "Child Maltreatment and Migraine," are available at its website.

Migraine Awareness Group: A National Understanding for Migraineurs (MAGNUM)
100 N. Union St.
Ste. B, Alexandria, VA 22314
phone: (703) 739-9384
fax: (703) 739-2432
e-mail: comments@ migraines.org
website: www .migraines.org

MAGNUM aims to assist migraine sufferers, their families, and their coworkers by educating the public about the nature of migraine disease as a serious biological disorder. By encouraging the US National Institutes of Health to fund research on migraine disease and other headache-related disorders, MAGNUM hopes to improve the quality of life for those who suffer from chronic maladies involving head pain. Currently, MAGNUM is advocating for legislation that recognizes intractable migraine as a disability. Its website includes links to discussion forums and dozens of essays and articles, including "Migraines During Childhood and Adolescence" and "Managing Your Career Despite Migraines."

Migraine Research Foundation (MRF)
300 E. Seventy-Fifth St.
Ste. 3K, New York, NY 10021
phone: (212) 249-5402
fax: (212) 249-5405
e-mail: contactmrf@ migraineresearch foundation.org
website: www.migraine researchfoundation.org

The MRF is committed to furthering the understanding of the causes and mechanisms of migraine, helping to develop improvements in treatment, and finding a cure. Established to provide hope and assistance for those suffering from migraine disease, the MRF is the only nonprofit organization in the United States that is dedicated solely to funding migraine research. The foundation's medical advisory board includes leading neurologists and scientists from across the country. Its website provides access to lists of adults' and children's headache centers, links to stories by migraine sufferers, and an archive of news articles, including "Some Headache Cures May Make the Pain Worse" and "Coping with Childhood Migraine."

Migraine Resource Network
website: http://migraine resourcenetwork.com

Supported by a grant from Endo Pharmaceuticals, the Migraine Resource Network is an educational initiative that provides information and tools that enhance therapeutic outcomes for migraine sufferers. Its website serves as an ongoing educational resource for lifelong learning to the migraine headache community—clinicians, patients, medical students, and families and friends of migraine sufferers as well. The network provides access to interactive multimedia educational programs such as "Headache Treatment Through the Ages" and links to the current issues of *Headache: The Journal of Head* and to the journal *Face Pain and Practical Pain Management.*

National Headache Foundation (NHF)
820 N. Orleans, Ste. 217, Chicago, IL 60610
phone: (888) 643-5552
(312) 274-2650
e-mail: info@head aches.org
website: www.head aches.org

The goal of the NHF is to research the causes of and treatments for headache and to improve the health care of headache sufferers. It provides educational and informational resources to sufferers' families, physicians who treat headache sufferers, health policy decision makers, and to the general public. The NHF maintains that headache should be perceived as a legitimate neurobiological disease and that sufferers deserve understanding and quality treatment. Its website offers a news archive and a "Tools for Sufferers" page that includes lists of frequently asked questions, information on patient assistance programs, and links to podcasts and case study videos.

National Institute of Neurological Disorders and Stroke (NINDS)
PO Box 5801
Bethesda, MD 20824
phone: (800) 352-9424
(301) 496-5751
website: www.ninds .nih.gov

A branch of the US National Institutes of Health, NINDS conducts, fosters, and guides research on the causes, prevention, diagnosis, and treatment of neurological disorders and stroke. It also provides grants-in-aid to public and private institutions and individuals in fields related to its areas of interest. Included at the NINDS website are an index of neurological disorders and a migraine information page.

National Pain Foundation (NPF)
website: www.national painfoundation.org

Established in 1998, the NPF is a nonprofit organization that works to enhance the functional recovery of people in pain by providing information, education, and support. The foundation provides a virtual community at its website, where resources are presented in a way that encourages patients to take an active role in the management of their chronic pain. A searchable database at the website includes support tools such as "Living with Chronic Pain" and lists of books, DVDs, and other resources focusing on headache and migraine.

US Food and Drug Administration (FDA)
10903 New Hampshire Ave.
Silver Spring, MD 20993
phone: (888)463-6332
website: www.fda.gov

An arm of the US Department of Health and Human Services, the FDA is responsible for assuring the safety, efficacy, and security of human and veterinary drugs, medical devices, and the food supply. The FDA is also responsible for advancing the public health by helping to speed innovations that make medicines more effective, safer, and more affordable and for helping the public get the science-based information they need regarding medicines and foods in order to maintain and improve their health. The searchable A–Z index at its website includes health articles and news releases, such as "FDA Approves Botox to Treat Chronic Migraine."

World Headache Alliance (WHA)
41 Welbeck St., W1G 8EA, London, UK
e-mail: info@w-h-a.org
website: www.w-h-a.org

The WHA is an international alliance of about forty national headache organizations from nearly thirty countries worldwide. The WHA partners with the International Headache Society and the World Health Organization with the goal of recognizing and relieving people affected by headache disorders everywhere in the world. The alliance also aims to increase the awareness of headache as a public health concern with profound social and economic impact. Its website includes links to headache resources and an archive of news and research articles such as "Placebo Is as Effective as Botox in Relieving Migraines."

FOR FURTHER READING

Books

Carolyn Bernstein, *The Migraine Brain: Your Breakthrough Guide to Fewer Headaches, Better Health.* New York: Pocket Books, 2009.

Roger K. Cady et al. *Managing Migraine: A Patient's Guide to Successful Migraine Care.* Toronto: Baxter, 2008.

Decheng Chen, *Single Point Acupuncture and Moxibustion for 100 Diseases.* Bloomington, IN: Trafford, 2010.

Valerie Delaune, *Trigger Point Therapy for Headaches and Migraines: Your Self-Treatment Workbook for Pain Relief.* Oakland, CA: New Harbinger, 2008.

Manfred Kaiser, *How the Weather Affects Your Health.* Sydney: Read How You Want, 2010.

Andrew Levy, *A Brain Wider than the Sky: A Migraine Diary.* New York: Simon and Schuster, 2010.

Dawn A. Marcus, *Ten Simple Solutions to Migraines.* Oakland, CA: New Harbinger, 2006.

Dawn A. Marcus and Philip A. Bain, *The Woman's Migraine Toolkit: Managing Your Headaches from Puberty to Menopause.* New York: DiaMedica, 2010.

Klaus Podoll and Derek Robinson, *Migraine Art: The Migraine Experience from Within.* Berkeley, CA: North Atlantic, 2009.

Teri Robert, *Living Well with Migraine Disease and Headaches.* New York: Harper, 2005.

Oliver Sacks, *Migraine.* New York: Vintage, 1999.

Periodicals and Internet Sources

Lesley Alderman, "Migraines Force Sufferers to Do Their Homework," *New York Times,* January 30, 2010.

Orly Avitzur, "Are You Making Your Headaches Worse?," *Consumer Reports,* October 2008. www.consumerreports.org.

Sherry Boschert, "Myths Connect Hypertension and Headaches," *Clinical Psychiatry News,* December 2009.

Doug Brunk, "Reassurance Is Potent Against Pediatric Migraines," *Family Practice News*, May 1, 2008.

Merle L. Diamond and Dawn Marcus, "Controversies in Headache Medicine: Migraine Prevention Diets," American Headache Society, May 2008. www.achenet.org/education.

Kathleen Doheny, "Migraines with Aura May Raise Stroke Risk," MedicineNet, August 25, 2010. www.medicinenet.com.

Amos Carvel Gipson, "What's the Difference Between a Headache and a Migraine?," *Tampa Tribune*, July 10, 2010.

HealthCentral, "Migraine Triggers," www.healthcentral.com/migraine/triggers.

Kayla Hoffman, "Seeking Balance: The Alternative of Chinese Medicine," *Natural Life*, September/October 2004. www.natural lifemagazine.com.

Michael Kahn, "Study Confirms Links Between Headaches, Weather," *Toronto Globe and Mail*, March 10, 2009.

Mary Brophy Marcus, "Migraines No Longer Minimized," *USA Today*, July 13, 2009.

Elaine Markowitz, "Getting to the Point on Pain Control," *St. Petersburg (FL)Times*, March 24, 2009.

Jessica Rae Patton, "Healing Headaches," *E— The Environmental Magazine*, July/August 2008.

Jennifer Bright Reich, "Could Botox Cure Your Headaches?," Everydayhealth, February 23, 2009. www.everydayhealth.com.

Steven Reinberg, "Botox May Prevent Some Migraines," *HealthDay*, February 15, 2010.

Teri Robert, "Anatomy of a Migraine," Help for Headaches & Migraine, February 3, 2010. www.helpforheadaches.com.

Michele G. Sullivan, "Magnetic Stimulation Device Effective Against Migraine Pain," *Clinical Psychiatry News*, April 2010.

Women's Health Weekly, "Link Between Migraines and Reduced Breast Cancer Risk Confirmed in Follow-Up Study," July 23, 2009.

Elaine Zablocki, "Triptans Lead Treatment Options for Migraine Management," *Managed Healthcare Executive*, March 2009.

INDEX

A

Abdominal migraine, 20
Accreditation Commission for
  Acupuncture and Oriental Medicine
  (ACAOM), 85
Acupoint 7, *74*
Acupuncture, 71, 72–75, *73*, 78, 79, 87,
  115
  personal account of migraineur on,
    112–116
  questions on effectiveness of, 80–83
  risk of misdiagnosis and, 88–92
  risks of, 83–84
Adolescents, migraines associated with
  alcohol/cigarette use by, 32–35
AHS (American Headache Society), 10, 37,
  60, 64
Alcohol, association with migraines in high
  schoolers, 32–35
Alexander technique, 124
Allergic rhinitis, effects on sinuses, *30*
Allergies, 27
Alternative Medicine Review (journal), 101
American College of Obstetricians and
  Gynecologists, 51
American Headache Society (AHS), 10, 37,
  60, 64
American Medical Association Council on
  Scientific Affairs, 81
American Migraine Study II, 28
Amitriptyline, 47
Analgesics, 22
  headaches associated with overuse of, 23,
    48–49

  in menstrually related migraine, 51
Anaphylactic reaction, 77
Anticonvulsants, 23
Antidepressants, 24
Archives of Internal Medicine (journal), 41
Aricept, 66
Asthma, 26–27
  migraine associated with, 30–31
Aura(s), 70
  migraine with, 19, 44–45
  migraine without, 20
  as phase in migraine attack, 18
Ayurveda practitioner, *100*

B

Barrett, Stephen, 77
Basilar-type migraine, 20
BenAvram, Debra, 59, 68
Berggoetz, Barb, 58
Bernstein, Carolyn, 97
Beta-blockers, 23, 48
  side effects of, 56*t*
Biofeedback, 65, 67–68, 101
Botox/Botox injections, 44, *44*, 106, 107,
  108, 123–124
Brain, hyper-excitability of, 97
A Brain Wider than the Sky (Levy), 9
Branch, David A., 110
Brookhiser, Richard, 122
Butterbur, 102
Byrne, Shannon, 110

C

Cady, Roger K., 25, 53, 106, 108

Calcitonin gene-related peptide (CGRP), 42, 62

Calcium channel blockers, 23–24, 48

Centers for Disease Control and Prevention (CDC), 35

CGRP (calcitonin gene-related peptide), 42, 62

Cigarette smoking, association with migraines in high schoolers, 32–35

Cluster headaches, 10–11
  symptoms of, 43

Coenzyme Q10 (CoQ10), 101–102

Consumer Reports (magazine), 89

Cutrer, F. Michael, 109

D
Dalton, Robert, 53

Department of Agriculture, US (USDA), 22

Diagnosis
  acupuncture and accuracy of, 88–92
  importance of accuracy in, 31

Diamond, Seymour, 60, 67

Diet, 17, 76

Dihydroergotamines, 66

Dodick, David, 38–39

Dowdle, Hillari, 96

E
Electroacupuncture, 73–75, 80

Ergot derivatives (ergotamines), 22, 49
  side effects of, 56t

Etters, Ashley, 67

F
Familial hemiplegic migraine (FHM), 20–21

FDA (US Food and Drug Administration), 61, 85

Feverfew, 102

FHM (familial hemiplegic migraine), 20–21

Five Elements theory, 71

Food and Drug Administration, US (FDA), 61, 85

G
Gale Health and Wellness Resource Center, 103

Godlasky, Anne, 41

Grazzi, Lisa, 65

Griffin, Sandie, 55

Gut Brain Therapy, 101

Guyuron, Bahman, 106–107, 109, 110

H
Hall, Harriet, 83

Headache (journal), 125

Headache Constorium, US, 48

Headache(s)
  cluster, 10–11, 43
  from medication overuse, 23, 48–49
  as phase in migraine attack, 18
  primary vs. secondary, 10
  severe, percent of adults with, 27
  sinus, 28–29, 43
  symptoms of, by type, 43
  TCM theory of, 70–71
  tension-type, 10, 32, 33, 43
  vascular, 16

Hemiplegic migraine, 20–21

Herbal medicine, 102
  Chinese, 75

Histamine, 33
  role in allergic rhinitis, 29–30

Holohan, Ellin, 36

Hong, Harry, 69

I
International Headache Society, 48

J
Janis, Jeffrey E., 106, 110

Jefferson, Thomas, 125

Journal of the American Chiropractic Association, 85

K
Kriegler, Jennifer S., 108, 110

L
Lancet (journal), 42
Levy, Andrew, 9–10
Lifestyle, 45
    changes in, 24
    regularity of, 75–76
Lipton, Richard B., 107, 108
Liver, in TCM theory of headaches, 70–71

M
Magnesium, 102
Mathew, Ninan, 12
Mauskop, Alexander, 44, 45
Maxalt, 44, 113–114
Medication overuse headache, 23, 48–49
Medications
    abortive (acute), 22–23, 104
    costs of, 47
    currently under study, 66
    group I *vs.* group II, 48
    most migraineurs are dissatisfied with, 52–57
    preventive, 23–24, 49, 64–65, 103
    side effects of, 47, 56t
Melzack, Ronald, 81
Menstruation-related migraine, 21, 49–51
Migraines, *14*
    age of highest occurrence, 69
    asthma associated with, 30–31
    costs to economy, 38, 55–56
    frequency of attacks, *98*
    in high schoolers, association with alcohol/cigarette use, 32–35
    lifestyle changes, and, 24, 45
    lifestyle factors, associated with, 33–35

model of mechanisms of, *50*
natural remedies are effective against, 96–104
new drugs are not always best choice, 46–51
obesity and, 24
other types of headache *vs.*, 11
pain of, 97
percent of adults with, *27*
personal account of treatment with acupuncture, 112–116
phases of, 18–19
prevalence of, 16, 23
rapid onset, 55
role of blood vessels in, *17*
source of term, 45
traditional Chinese medicine (TCM) offers effective therapies for, 69–76
triggers of, 12, 16–17, 33, 71, 97, 118–119
types of, 19–21, 70
underdiagnosis of, 10, 28
See also Diagnosis; Treatment(s); Lifestyle
Migraineur(s) (migraine sufferers)
    new drugs for, may help, 41–45, 58–68
    percent reporting coexisting allergies, 28
    personal account of, 117–121
    stigma faced by, 36–39
Milde-Busch, Astrid, 33, 35
Mohammad, Yousef, 45, 64

N
Naproxen sodium, 51
National Certification Commission for Acupuncture and Oriental Medicine (NCCAOM), 85
National Council Against Health Fraud (NCAHF), 86, 87
National Headache Foundation (NHF), 53, 66, 106

National Institute of Neurological
  Disorders and Stroke, 15
National Institutes of Health (NIH), 15, 71,
  87–88, 89–90
National Migraine Treatment Survey, 57
Natural remedies, are effective against
  migraines, 96–104
Nervous system, role in migraines, 26
Neurology (journal), 28, 102
Neurontin, 66
NHF (National Headache Foundation), 53,
  66, 106
NIH (National Institutes of Health), 15, 71,
  87–88, 89–90
Nonsteroidal anti-inflammatory drugs
  (NSAIDs), 22, 48
  side effects of, 56t

O
Obesity, Fitness & Wellness Week (journal),
  32
Occipital nerve stimulation (ONS), 65–66
Ophthalmoplegic migraine, 21
Opiates, 104
  side effects of, 56t
Oral contraceptives, 49–50, 119

P
Park, Jung E., 37
Patient Health International, 113
Plastic and Reconstructive Surgery (journal),
  106
Plastic surgery
  can ease migraines, 105–110
  survey on results of, 109
PR Newswire, 52
Prochlorperazine, 66
Propranolol, 47

Q
Qi Gong, 76, 78–79

R
Rapoport, Alan, 42

S
Safer, Jeanne, 42, 44, 45
Saint Louis, Catherine, 105
Salinas, Patti, 64–65
Sampson, Wallace, 88
Science Daily (website), 38
Sensenig, James, 97–98
Serotonin, 22, 24
Silberstein, Stephen, 42, 61, 62, 65
Sinus headache, 28–29
  symptoms of, 43
Sinuses, effects of allergic rhinitis on, 30
Sinusitis, 29
Staccato device, 66
Status migrainosus, 21
Stress, 16, 45
  regulating, 24, 67–68
Sumatriptan, 66
Surveys
  on headaches in adolescents, 33–34
  on migraine attacks/treatment, 53–55
  on results of plastic surgery, 109
Symptoms
  of headaches, by type, 43
  of migraine, 11, 60

T
Tai Ji Quan, 76
TCM. *See* Traditional Chinese medicine
Telcagepant, 62
Tension-type headaches (TTH), 10, 32,
  33
  symptoms of, 43
Thermogram, 14
Tietjen, Gretchen E., 47, 49–50, 51
TMS (transcranial magnetic stimulator),
  59–60, 62–63, 63

Tonabersat, 62

Topiramate (Topomax), 48
side effects of, 47, 56t

Traditional Chinese medicine (TCM)
effectiveness has not been proved, 77–95
offers effective therapies for migraineurs, 69–76

Transcranial magnetic stimulator (TMS), 59–60, 62–63, 63

Treatment(s)
simple immediate, 21–22
strategies for, 98–101
See also Medications; specific treatments

Treximet, 48

Trigeminal nerve, 12

Trigeminal nerve system, 42

Triptans, 22, 43, 51
drawbacks of, 61–62
first FDA approval of, 61
side effects of, 56t

TTH. See Tension-type headaches

Tyramine, 33

U

Ulett, George A., 81

W

Wachter, Kerri, 46

Wall, Patrick D., 81

Weather, migraines related to, 125

WebMD (website), 120

WHO (World Health Organization), 23, 35, 51, 88

Women
menstruation-related migraines in, 18, 49–51
percent reporting migraines related with menstrual cycle, 120
prevalence of migraines in, 17, 59, 113

World Health Organization (WHO), 23, 35, 51, 88

Y

Ying-Yang, imbalance in, 70

Z

Zang-Fu organ system, 70

Zolmitriptan, 66